Mongolian Empire

History from Beginning the Mongols Empire

(A Step by Step Captivating Guide to a Remarkable Genghis Khan & the Mongol Empire)

Ernest Lyon

Published By **Jordan Levy**

Ernest Lyon

Mongolian Empire: History from Beginning the Mongols Empire (A Step by Step Captivating Guide to a Remarkable Genghis Khan & the Mongol Empire)

ISBN 978-1-9995502-9-5

Legal & Disclaimer

Table Of Contents

Chapter 1: Rags to Riches

A single of the most remarkable features of the Empire Genghis Khan was to be able to conquer and consolidate is the humble beginnings. The great conquerors of history generally gained having a head start in the beginning of their career. Alexander the Great had a nearly perfect military apparatus from his father, who was the greatest modernizer of his Macedonian army. Julius Caesar had the benefit of a long-standing warrior community that was devoted to conquering and expanding to his side. Napoleon could draw upon the power of a nation which, although poor and in the process of being revolutionized but was nevertheless one of the most ancient and most powerful of Europe. Genghis Khan was not a part of these. The place he started from was an unorganized group of nomad warrior tribes that were formed into federations, but all extremely independent and nearly completely hostile to any non-natives. This would take a strong spirit and a lot of grit to transform the steppe warriors into one of the most formidable combat forces.

The harsh terrain breeds hard-headed men Steppes in Mongolia in which Genghis Khan was raised, is a prime example of the perfect place. In the "sea of grass" was home to the Mongols who were tribesmen who were fiercely independent and moved from place to place seeking food sources and other forage. They were famous archers and riders, and horses was considered as a symbol of respect in Mongolian tradition as a key element of a person's life as a means of transportation in a country which was arid and soaring, as well as foods were in the form of dried horseflesh and fermented cow's milk, and milk curds which were all part that were part of Mongolian cuisine. Mongolian diet. The way they lived their lives was simple and akin to the hunter-gatherer lifestyle and warriors from tribes. Even their pious rituals, that revolved on the sky, appear quaint in the present day.

The Mongols were accustomed to extreme difficulties and believed to have the ability to endure long hours riding in the saddle and relying entirely on the scraps of food as well as blood of their own horses that were the same as their own and, in some cases, even stronger. The soft life was viewed in Mongolia because it was both sexy and unthinkable people who lived the practice (i.e. non-Mongolian religions) were considered to be effeminate and insecure. In the harsh landscape in which Genghis Khan came to be between the years 1160-1170 A.D., not far from the present-day Mongolian capital city of Ulaan-Bataar. The sources for his life in the early years are sporadic and unreliable since it wasn't until Genghis Khan was in contact with people with a rich writing tradition that his story became more reliable however, historians are capable of assembling a lot of his youth and his early accomplishments with some degree of accuracy.

It is the Onon River in Mongolia, the area in which Genghis Khan was born, and lived his entire life.

Genghis Khan was born under Temujin as his birth name He was the child of Yesugei Khan of the Borjigin tribe as well as Holeun from the Olkhunut The latter is believed to be named in honor of an Tatar warlord who Yesugei defeated during the battle. The third son of Yesugei (his first was with Holeun) He had two brothers older than him named Hasar and Haciun. they were later joined by his younger sibling, Temuge. Temulen was also his sister named Temulen and two half-brothers: Behter as well as Belgutei. There's no evidence of the actual appearance that Temujin was like. Most images of him found in the archives have been created post-his death and the accounts of his life tend to be laced with symbolism, and reflect mythological and prophetic visions of an enemy conqueror much as much as the appearance of Temujin's. The most accurate and complete description of his appearance comes in the work of Persian historian Rashid-ad-Din which, somewhat paradoxically declares him to be large in stature, with eyes that were green and red. These were not traits of a common Mongol during the time however it's possible that Temujin was a person with these traits as they have been observed in Mongolian people even to the present day.

Many omens are believed be associated with the time of his birth, but they are likely to be unsubstantiated. One of the most well-known ones says that Temujin arose from the womb of Holeun with the blood clot that was encased within his fist. This is an old omen that indicated that he was going to be an emperor. The fate however wasn't immediately evident because at the time Temujin aged around six older and his mother Holeun was a mother to a second child, Temuge. According to Mongol traditions, this was Temuge who was to inherit more of Yesugei's fortune and status being the youngest son of the ruler is traditionally inherited. This tradition, obviously stands in sharp contrast with Western tradition that the son with the highest rank inherit the estate.

Although the Yesugei family did not plan to allow Temujin to succeed him however, he didn't intend to make him penniless, also, so a suitable wedding was scheduled to him at a young age. This was a common practice for the Mongols. As young as nineteen, He was taken by the father of his family to Onggirat tribe, which was located nearby. Onggirat tribe. There he was welcomed with the families of Borte whom he believed was set to be his bride. In accordance with tradition, her family was responsible for his care until when he was 12 years old, at which point the expectation was that he'd get married. If they were to marry, Borte would bring Temujin the dowry of a significant amount in exchange in exchange for being married to a son of Khan however, until that time Temujin was to remain in the service of the Borte family.

The majority of his training was already completed in this time, as it was considered to be an adult at the age of 12 and, at the age of 12, Temujin already had the skills of a hunter, wrestler, archer and hunter. In the event of fate his skills would become important to him and his family over the next few years as even while he sat and was watching his father's horse disappear and his mother saunter away, the beginning in a long life filled with it was nearing.

In his return journey after delivering Temujin back to the Onggirat Yesugei was greeted by a large group of traveling Tatars his old enemies. He was willing to share a meal together. In the course of the battle, however they Tatars took poison to him and Yesugei was killed shortly afterwards. As news of the incident arrived at Temujin's home, he swiftly quit the Onggirat and headed home when he appeared to the Borjigin, and declared that he was going to take over Yesugei's position as Khan. It was no surprise that the teenage boy was ridiculed by the Borjigin and was told that he was not old enough and untested to step into Yesugei's role. A gruesome but typical scenario, he and his mother and his siblings, as well as his half-brothers and sister were abandoned by Borjigin who left them to struggle by themselves, with nothing other than their clothes shoulders during the cold winter of the steppes, without horses or any support from a tribe.

The rapid change of the things was made more dramatic due to the fact that the tribal system was an individual's Mongol tribe was the most important thing for his.

Without it, he became an outcast, unimportant at risk, and not only of starvation in the harsh grassy sand, but also of enslavement to a consequence-free slave or even death. Temujin lived this way for many years, barely making it through as an outcast but the constant menace of starvation always looking at him And it was during this period that his mother instilled one of the principles which would eventually guide Temujin's upcoming policies The tribe was the only thing it was, and the alliance was essential for escaping the life of an outcast. Holeun and her kids lived by surviving on the remnants of tribes from other tribes and the hunt they were able to get and dress themselves in skins of animals and living in a shelter they constructed themselves. These were obviously difficult times however, it was in the time of hardship that Temujin's inherent resourcefulness and drive to be a leader made him the actual chief of the family and was a role for that he had to compete with his older half-brothers Behter and Belgutei whom they viewed as rebel. Temujin however was more powerful than Belgutei and Behter, and showed that at preteen, he was old and brutal in the past in the event that he killed Belgutei after the elder boy refused to surrender his hunted animals in exchange for a common pot. Even though they were exiles, it appears like even the tiniest incidents of the renegade family of Temujin have attracted the attention of Mongol tribe, as this murder appears to have attracted attention and was the very first tassel that would later become that later to become a terrifying image.

The year 1182 saw Temujin's family's solitude was abruptly broken when the Tayichiud the local tribe which shared ancestral ties and the Borjigin and were friends of Yesugei and seized Temujin during the course of a raid, and forced him to become slave. Temujin had to face difficulties that were more severe than the ones that he faced in his exile, and spent the majority of his time in a movable stock that was like an ox's yoke. The situation was so dire, the guard was sympathized enough with his situation to assist him in escaping the Taychiud. Temujin was freed from his captivity in the darkness and was able to hide under a riverbank, only to remove his yoke. It was a crucial element of his fame, and his shrewd getaway from Taychiud resulted in him gaining an impressive amount of fame among the plains in which such acts of piracy were viewed with awe.

After his escape, Temujin met with Jelme and Borchu Two warriors who agreed to join the service of Temujin and to support his claim to the title of The Khan of Borjigin. They were welcomed by Jamukha an aspiring young Mongol nobleman who was father of the tribe's Khan at the period. Jamukha ended up becoming Temujin's bloodbrother and close friend. After gaining confidence due to his rise to fame in the world, Temujin made a formal appearance before the Onggirat in his 16th year and demanded that the father of Borte honor the promises he signed with Yesugei, and grant his hand to marry Borte as a gesture that the older man was honorable enough and wise enough to accept. Even though the wedding was planned and arranged, it appears that Temujin had really fallen in love with Borte and she was his sole queen throughout time. Even though there were other wives, which was what was the norm and he was never allowed to succeed Borte.

Soon after the wedding Temujin, along with his followers took vows of loyalty in the name of Toghrul Khan, the Khan of the

Kerait which was a formidable union made up of Mongol tribes. Toghrul was Yesugei's bloodbrother It was as a result of the bond and his rising fame to Temujin, that he took his vow.

Genghis Khan and Toghrul Khan. Illustration taken from the 15th century Jami'al-tawarikh manuscript

Temujin will never regret making the vow because the next day Borte was abducted by the Merkits an alleged rival of the union, and was made the wife of one of their fighters. Temujin was devastated however, Toghrul Khan, according to reports, gave his the sum of 200,000 (almost definitely an overstated amount) of his troops and ordered him to defeat the Merkits and, by so accomplishing, regain Borte back. Toghrul clearly recognized that Temujin's potential as a leader who was a natural leader, so he accepted him as a friend and encouraged him to seek assistance from his blood brother Jamukha and had made it to the position of Khan of the mighty Jadaran tribe. Meanwhile, Temujin as well as Borte were enjoying their marriage.

Temujin's very first major war was brief bloody, but extremely effective. The Merkits were nearly destroyed in several battles, and Temujin could reclaim Borte without injury, but the rumor that he was according to the reports, completely unharmed. Borte's son from her first marriage, Jochi, was inconveniently born just nine months following her heartbreaking experience. Even while she as well as Temujin have remained steadfast in refusing to admit his parentage, doubt hung over the young man throughout his entire life. However that campaign against the Merkits could also be the source of a conflict between her and Jamukha despite their prior relationship as blood brothers The rift was to become a growing rivalry.

Alongside getting the wife back his victory in the battle against the Merkits led to Temujin having a huge amount of respect, authority and admirers, and the latter began to be seen as a real warlord in his own in his own right. In the presence of Toghrul's approval and support, Temujin launched an operation in the subsequent time to unite the tribal groups in Central Mongolia under his control. The tribal groups of central Mongolia as opposed to the vast unions to west and east had a largely fractured society, which allowed Temujin the ability to take them in pieces despite the fact that they were brave warriors. Temujin was adept at playing the game of alliance as also, convincing certain tribes to give their blood to him, and pitting a few tribes against one another.

Temjuin was also able to implement policy that was radical in every way. In the past, tribal members who were defeated would be looking forward to a time of slavery, summary execution or diaspora. However, Temujin could be the reason, as the fact that he was a slave and an outcast and was a slave, embraced the lost within his own tribe, perhaps even the idea of having his mother Holeun to adopt orphans from war as her own to create children of the tribe who had lost half of them. It was a kind and compassionate way of life that earned him the respect and respect of those who might otherwise slam the man. And when defeated warriors realized the warrior would accept them as his own and offer them an equal share of the spoils that would follow triumph, they came to his flag. Establishing a method of advancement and rank within the Temujin army which did not depend upon blood or family, however, but on merit alone made it clear that the generals and captains were among the most skilled that the Mongols could create, as they established their name and made them last by using only swords.

The year 1190 saw Temujin succeed in bringing the whole Central Mongolia under his control and bringing its various, tribal factions into one militarily and administrative entity. Temujin was also the father of at least three times as many, given that his wife was the mother to his sons Chagatai, Ogadai and Tolui between 1190 and 1190. It's not clear if any others died during infancy or the number of daughters he was blessed with, in any case, which is an sign that girls were less crucial to chroniclers as sons.

Temujin's achievements wasn't unnoticed and it started to concern Toghrul and his family, who believed that Temujin would remain loyal to him in spite of the fact

Temujin was rapidly becoming an extremely powerful warlord with "radical" policies that made his people more loyal as opposed to the norm. Toghrul's anxiety was further aggravated by his envious son Sengum who was fervently angry at Temujin's. Sengum believed that temujin had taken over his position within his father's heart He was quick to pour poison into the ear of Toghrul to warn Toghrul that Temujin was soon to become powerful enough to take over the former president. Sengum recommended that Toghrul be rid of Temujin immediately It appears that Sengum as well as his gang attempted to take over Temujin's personal life at this point. It was almost certain that the attempt took place through Toghrul's implicit consent and Temujin was certainly aware of this, since their relationship initially pleasant, began to become acrimonious. To try to restore their relationship Temujin was so bold as to propose to wed Jochi with one of the daughters of Toghrul, however Toghrul declined. This was an egregious and deliberate insult, but likely a result of men's doubts concerning Jochi's family which caused Temujin to become angry. If there was no amicable resolution of the conflict the possibility of conflict.

Toghrul was concerned about Temujin's newly established Mongol union and also of his commanding skills and strategist, therefore he tried to even the playing field by aligning himself to Jamukha. Although Jamukha retained respect and love towards his blood brother both were adversaries for a long time. Even if it was to be the first significant clash between them. In the end, Jamukha proved to be not as a dependable ally for Toghrul the way he had been in the case of Temujin The two quickly splintered, and their differences aggravated due to the fact that a large number of the most important tribes believed to be in their newly-formed coalition renounced Temujin. Toghrul as well as Jamukha were defeated however, even although Jamukha along with a large majority of his supporters managed to leave however, the Kerait as an autonomous federation was dissolved. They were then incorporated in the newly formed Mongol union, and their survivors went onto increase the number of Temujin's vast army.

Temujin was focusing his attention on Jamukha and his family, who had left west to the land of the Naiman Federation, as well as all of his troops and supporters. The Naimans led by Kuchlug together with the few who remains of the Merkits formed the Kurultai (council of Khans) and appointed Jamukha as the Naimans' Gur Khan (Great leader). Temujin is well-known, and with his goals of Mongolian unification, couldn't avoid a insult to the face and he then marched over Jamukha along with his new allies. Before the battle even began the ranks of his army were increased by hundreds of deserters who believed that they would gain from serving in the new meritocratic army. One of them was Subotai, who was a general and an infamous soldier. He was also the Jelme's brother, and among Temujin's commanders as well as his first supporters.

Another unusual practice was that the army of Temujin accepted deserters and treated them more favorably than captured warriors who had been defeated adversaries. Deserters were greeted with open arms as warriors who had been defeated and enemies were for the first time, savagely treated as they received the status of being "measured against the linchpin" and were made to pass the wheel of a wagon. If they were taller than the wagon wheel (meaning they were fully grown and not yet stooped by age), they were beheaded, ostensibly to prevent tribal rivalries that might be nourished by not-easily-indoctrinated adults.

Temujin fought with Jamukha in a half-dozen combats. Although none were decisive, Jamukha nevertheless suffered several losses over the course of time that led to his apathetic followers to turn Jamukha to Temujin 1206. The move was a disaster, and Temujin declared that he was not going to tolerate with those who were not loyal to his troops was able to have Jamukha's traitors to be executed publicly. The king also offered to extend the friendship he had with Jamukha and promised him a position with respect within his ranks, however Jamukha who was humiliated by the loss, instead pleaded to be executed in a dignified manner. In accordance with Mongolian custom, a hygienic execution should be without blood so Temujin complied with his request.

The battle was far from ended with the

defeat of Jamukha, but the battle was

nearly over. The remaining Merkits were

defeated in a piecemeal fashion by Subotai. He was promoted to general in the Temujin army, and swiftly proving the faith put in him, as well as his image of a competent commander that he gained within the enemies of Temujin. Kuchlug, the Kahlu of the Naiman Federation, Kuchlug, realized that his hope was now gone, and fled to the west, to the territories of the Kara-Khitai Khanate and remained in the Kara-Khitai Khanate, which was in its own and hostile towards Temujin. They must have been feeling lonely as they were essentially completely alone when it came to preserving their

sovereignty. Within just several years,

either hook or by steal Temujin unified the Naimans, Merkits as well as the Tatars as well as the Uyghurs as well as the Keraits into one Mongol Federation, something that was unheard of before in the history of. In a kuruldai, sometime around the year 1206 A.D., Temujin was declared by the Khans as Genghis Khan the great Khan of all Mongols.

Genghis Khan was declared Khagan among all Mongols. Illustration taken from the 15th century Jami' al tawarikh manuscript

After having accomplished what no one else in his time believed was feasible, Genghis could have been happy with the results he accomplished. Yet, he was not accomplished. His promises to his countrymen additional things, such as the plundering of China and promised to fulfill his promise.

Chapter 2: The Terror from the Steppes

There may be earlier connections with Chinese the dynasties via Toghrul Khan as well as the Chinese were definitely aware and perhaps concerned about the activities of Temujin His involvement in the issues of the constantly battling Chinese dynasties started in 1205 as a band of rebellious Mongols of the Kerait tribe sought refuge with the Xi Xia Dynasty in what is now North-West China. Since the Xi Xia had offered Keraits aid, Keraits assistance, Genghis launched an attack over their territory and forced some local nobles to accept Genghis as their supreme ruler. At the time Genghis was in the process of fighting Jamukha and unifying Mongolia which is why the initial invasion into Chinese territories was repelled.

When he was able to unite with the Mongols However, Genghis returned to the realms of Xi Xia in 1207, and this time, he returned in a fury. The fortress was quickly destroyed by Genghis. of Wulahai which was one of the most important military Xi Xia garrisons, after taking by deceit and later taking over the rest of the area. It was an ebb in the conflict between 1207 and 1209 however, hostilities rekindled in 1209 when Genghis began an offensive with an army of approximately 100,000 Mongol cavalry and infantry, at the heart of it were the feared horse archers. combatants that traditional forces encountered a major challenge. The double-curved bows they used were incredibly strong despite their small dimensions, nearly as powerful than English longbows. Furthermore, they could fire them as quickly on the horse as they could do from the feet. Equally important, archers on horses were so adept with horses that they were able to take off at a speed and smother slow-moving formations with an arrow storm prior to veering swiftly away from an attack. They could be devastating in open fields and had the ability to take out any adversary regardless of how well armored because heavy armor caused them to be slower in their maneuvers. The Mongol cavalry proved useless when defense of fortifications in the attack, or fortifications, and also the Xia took advantage on this and seek using this advantage to the fullest extent.

In spite of their boldness, and their ability to have over 150,000 soldiers, Genghis successfully seized Wulahai in 1209 but this time with a vengeance The Xi-Xia was evidently had learned nothing from the previous siege of Wulahai's fortress. Genghis then led his troops through into the Huang River into the Xi Xia central region and then seized the capital city, Zhongxing. The Mongol army was able to encircle Zhongxing, cutting access routes to supply, but the army soon became stuck. Genghis Khan was not averse to fortifications as large as Zhongxing that had huge bastions brimming with catapults, artillery and other and bowmen equipped with crossbows that repeatedly recurred. The Zhongxing fortifications were massive and daunting obstacle that required sophisticated and advanced siege engines in order to lessen. The walls were not moved by an escalade. Genghis required siege towers in order to get them, catapults, and Trebuchets to pound a hole as well as his troops had no technical know-how for building them, nor the expertise to deploy these effectively should they have.

In a state of confusion, Genghis devised an ingenius plan; he'd use the massive manpower available in his arsenal to divert and dam the Huang River, thereby flooding Zhongxing and causing its surrender. However, his ambitious plan failed, and even though Genghis succeeded in damming the waterway, he was fail to divert it in the intended direction. Actually, he was able to accidentally destroy the Mongol camp due to the sudden roiling of the river. The magnitude of his task convinced the Xi Xia leader Li Anquan to give Zhonxing to him. He had been convinced that nothing could hinder Genghis from getting his way. Li Anquan accepted one of his daughters to marry, along with other tokens of respect and a huge quantity of tribute that quickly washed into the hungry Mongol army. He also accepted the existence of an Mongol army in Zhonxing. One fell swoop and Genghis was able to reduce Xi Xia along with its riches and powerful army into a state of client.

Even with Genghis's sensational victory Genghis's other Chinese states didn't seem to pay attention except to be ecstatic in the humiliation of a competitor. In the year 1210, Jin strong state situated to the south Xi Xia that had long engaged in maintaining Mongolian tribes unstable to keep the unification of their tribes and unified, sent an embassy to Genghis. The ambassador announced that the new Jin Emperor had been declared in a sly manner, and advised to Genghis give tokens of respect to the Jin as his lord. Unsurprisingly, Genghis was not pleased. However the top Jin officials made use of the embassy's defection towards Genghis and encourage Genghis to fight the Jin and his comrades, Genghis resisted the advice of these officials due to fear of being a victim to treachery. His response to the Jin ambassador was to shout at his feet, then run away. That would mean war.

The year 1211 was the time that Genghis Khan called a Kurultai in order to declare the outbreak of war. That was the year that he sprang his massive army, which numbered approximately 100,000 soldiers, to fight the Jin who were said to include as many as one million soldiers in their armour themselves. Genghis Khan's army consisted of cavalry. They were with armored heavy cavalry as well as archers on horses, and was not a commissariat nor a supply train. It was extremely mobile.

The Mongols began by engaging in a series of undecisive battles against far superior (around 400,000 soldiers) Chinese forces which, while not critical to the final outcome of war nevertheless gave commanders such as Jebe the Arrow, Muqali and Subotai plenty of opportunity to establish themselves in the presence of Tolui and Ogadai who were Genghis's two brothers who were given with their own armies.

Then eventually, it was decided that the Mongol army moved to the narrow defile of Badger Pass in the Zhangjiakou area. The Mongols typically were scourging and cutting across the entire west side from Badger Pass, which was the only natural defensive spot that was to the west of the sprawling Zhongdu city. Zhongdu (modern Beijing, and the home of the Jin the Emperor). Heisilie Hushashu General Heisilie Hushashu, who was in charge of the Jin troops, who thanks to an urgent call-up from each town and garrison within the Jin domains, now had a total of more than 500,000 soldiers, understood what he was doing: Badger Pass would negate the benefits of Mongol ability to maneuver by forcing archers of the horse to let go of their weapons and ride the horses inside their own boundaries. The result would turn the battle into a fight between hand and hand that favors Jin's strategy and weapons.

Illustration of fight scenes in Badger Pass

But, at this point the Mongols began to arm them using Chinese steel cuirasses as well as making their own. Moreover, their cavalry was well-armed and adequately protected in hand-to-hand combat. Additionally, prior to start of the battle, Genghis, displaying magnificent ability to plan, sent his unarmed soldiers to ascend the peaks in Badger Pass and encircle the enemies' army. They attacked them from behind as Genghis made progress on the major part of his forces to the Pass. Despite having no room to maneuver and maneuver, the Mongol soldiers proved superior against the Jin professional soldiers and conscripts, and the in-circled Jin army completely defeated, and the scattered survivors being snatched by the raging Mongol cavalry over 30 miles. The Jin general left for Zhongdu in China, where he killed the Jin Emperor and assumed the control of the city. He named his son Wanyang Xun as the new Emperor.

In the meantime, Genghis detached a force under Jebe to attack and harass Manchuria which they then seized Zhongdu, which was the capital of Shenyang. The year 1212 was the date of their capture, and even though Genghis was wounded during the time but his fellow Mongols were the rulers of Manchuria and ready to confront Zhongdu its own city in the middle of the Jin central region. In spite of some of his units losing to an unarmed section made up of Jin troops, Genghis and his generals tore the Jin forces on the field into shards and destroyed the now not defended Chinese plains prior to capturing Zhongdu at the time of 1214.

Another time, Genghis found it difficult to build in a Chinese stronghold. Through a prolonged siege Genghis failed to lower the walls of the city, however their situation became so dire that defense forces were ultimately driven to food insecurity and began to eat their dead. In addition their commander Heishilie Husashu was killed and his life. Then the Jin gave up Zhongdu and also agreed to offer Genghis an enormous tribute such as has not been witnessed before, and Genghis was also presented with a princess. Jin gave him the bride of his dreams. Content, happy and confident that he was the superior leader, Genghis withdrew his army.

Convinced that Zhongdu was not an impregnable fortress he had imagined and Wanyang Xun retreated Zhongdu Jin capital out of the destruction of the Mongols towards the city of Kaifeng in the south of Kaifeng. In 1215, one of the Jin forces defected from Genghis's side. Apparently without a hint of instigation, they began an assault on Zhongdu. Profiting from the situation, Genghis sent a fresh Mongol army to Zhongdu in 1215, and the city was destroyed ruthlessly during the month of May that year. Zhongdu was destroyed. Zhongdu as well as the surrender to one of the more powerful Jin military units that fought in the vicinity caused a break in the Jin opposition, and over the subsequent years (1215-1217) The Mongol army swept up the remnants of their resistance in the vast majority of northwestern Jin regions, and then added them to the growing Mongol Empire.

The depiction of Mongol cavalry combating Jin warriors

While the cleaning up of the mess took years to complete, Genghis was now effectively controlling the majority of the area In addition to increasing his territory as well as a huge quantity of riches,

Genghis and his army have also gained an abundance of knowledge and experience. Subjugating west China provided better armor as well as improved blacksmithing techniques for Mongol warriors. There was also a large number of logisticians and supply specialists that could supply Genghis's army with communications and supplies stretching many miles. There were also thousands, perhaps hundreds of extremely experienced Chinese soldiers who were able to know how to build and operate battle weapons of the kind that the Mongols were never previously. A fortress no matter the size or sophistication it was, could ever meet their formidable capabilities.

In return to the Mongolian region with an army loaded with the bounty of their petty robbery, but exhausted from an entire decade of bloody combat, Genghis turned his attention to other areas. In the to the west of Mongols were more of a grassy sea that stretched to unimaginable boundaries, yet in charge was the massive and bloody Khara-Kitai Khanate. Khara-Kitai, the horse nomads as those of the Mongols were led by Kuchlug, Genghis Khan's erstwhile opponent. Kuchlug was the one who had taken over the throne from the Khan who first offered him as well as the broken remnants of his army refuge as he fled west to escape Genghis's vengeance. The Khara-Kitai were oppressed by a ruthless and treacherous leader, who had shown his disdain for the king of Genghis the Great Khan, and so as they were concerned, as far as Genghis the Great Khan's interests were concerned,, they would be next on his list. But, Genghs knew that he would not be able to demand much from his troops that was exhausted but extremely content by the wealth they collected in the ravaging of the Jin the heartland. Not to forget the enormous sum of money they Chinese were willing to pay. The majority of Mongol troops wanted to relish the rewards from their decade of battle, and would like to be retired completely. Other soldiers were with garrison duties in China's Jin or Xi Xia territories. But Genghis maintained a substantial quantity of troops which included his most young and courageous, in fact. there were fresh army of warriors with training who were children when the first time he went away to China. Genghis was also awash with eager generals that longed for greater progress and more wealth.

At the end of the day, Genghis picked Jebe who had excelled in his campaigns in the battle against Xi Xia and the Jin and the Jin, to lead a tiny group of soldiers to the Khara-Kitai region. This was an enormous risk because Genghis was aware that Jebe was unable to take on the larger force of

Kuchlug who were just as skilled at fighting steppes just like Genghis's troops. He was however, confident of his younger general's wisdom and Jebe didn't disappoint him. Instead of attempting to confront Kuchlug's troops head-on, Jebe took on the guerrilla war, striking quickly before disappearing from the steppes, increasing in strong. Chiefs of Kuchlug who were more shrewd were aware that should Jebe lost, they'd most likely incur the curse of Great Khan, and would have to face the vast Mongol army later on and retreated to the side of Jebe.

Jebe's army had grown enough by 1218 that Jebe was at a point of confidence to fight Kuchlug in battle. The resultant battle that took place close to Kashgar which was an absolute catastrophe for Kuchlug who was defeated and was forced to flee in fear for his life. He did not escape for long. Kuchlug along with a small group of his wounded supporters were pursued in the aftermath of battle by Jebe and his army following the fight and was shot dead, ending the Khara-Kitai Khanate which later became part of the Mongol Empire. Genghis Khan had now been ruled by an enormous region, stretching across Beijing up to the present day Afghanistan.

According to all indications, Genghis Khan could have had a choice of putting his foot down. He achieved his objective of bringing all steppe tribes and people together, and bringing the tribes of warriors and confederations of the grassy sea under his banner. Apart from establishing an entirely new and powerful Mongol people, Mongol additionally humbled the Chinese who had mingled with Mongol issues for a long time, and reduced a large portion of their west-coast kingdoms to being conquered vassals.

Genghis could have rest on his achievements and revelled in the riches he made however it wasn't to be. In the west, Genghis's domains were now bordered by those that of Shah of Khwarezm the powerful leader who held all the area that ran from to the Arabian Peninsula to Afghanistan and south until the Himalayas and was set to commit the greatest error of his lifetime.

Chapter 3: Total War

The Shah of Khwarezm, Ala-ud-Din Muhammad, was, by all indications, an aggressive man. The Shah had been confronted by the caliph in Baghdad the notional ruler who was expecting an "gift" in return for being able to confirm his appointment as Sultan. This was something Ala-ud-Din could not see fit to offer. There was plenty of reason to be wary of Genghis Khan as well as the Mongols due to the fact that he was a Mongol ambassador from Zhongdu who told his firsthand about the Mongol crimes committed in the city. Therefore, he was incredibly skeptical when news came through that Genghis Khan was seeking to diplomatically make an alliance offer to Khwarezm as well as his fears were further strengthened after Genghis was able to send a caravan to Khwarezm in the year 1218. The caravan, a trading mission of around five hundred people, mainly composed of Muslim vassals to show a sign in respect for the Khwarezm faith it reached Otrar, the capital city. Otrar. The Governor of Otrar was an arrogant, egocentric man identified as Inalchuq who was a shrewd man, judged that the small group of Mongols who were accompanying the caravan Spies and sent the Mongols in jail in addition to seizing the goods of the caravan.

It's safe to say that Genghis Khan was not thrilled with this response. Mongol couriers were able to travel extremely quickly during this time and changed horses in specially well-established waystations. They could travel more than 100 miles per day. As a result, news got to Genghis back in the steppe fairly rapidly. When he heard the information, Genghis dispatched an urgent diplomatic team consisting of two Mongol officials and a Muslim (as an offer of support to the

Shah's religion) to appear before the Shah and request for the freedom of Mongols taken captive by the caravan as well the immediate detention of Inalchuq and the transfer to Genghis Khan's court for the offense. Ala-ud-Din However, he exploded in a fury over his insulting demands made by an amoral barbaric half-way across the globe He ordered to have the heads of both Mongol ambassadors to be shaved off as insults. The Muslim was killed and his head was handed over to two dignitaries who had their heads shaved, and they were then hurriedly returned to where they came from. Others in the caravan were also executed.

Genghis responded to this deliberate insult and display of barbarism in predictable anger. Genghis amassed the most powerful army he'd ever commanded in his career, totalling 200 000 soldiers based on an elite group consisting of light and heavy horses and cavalry, as well as support units that included Chinese medical specialists, siege warfare and military engineers, as well as the commissariat and siege train that contained all kinds of crossbows, from massive mortars to catapults as well as Trebuchets that could launch gunspowder-filled bombs. Genghis summoned the most skilled generals, Subotai Jebe, Mukali, Jelme and his brother Hasar as well as his children Jochi Chagatai and Jochi Tolui. They marched across the steppe. He stood at the frontier of Khwarezm.

Prior to the invasion, Genghis split up his army into several units that gave them greater mobility. A particular army, led by Jochi and comprising approximately 25000 men, was sent straight at the Shah himself the moment they entered the field to frighten the Shah and possibly taking him down, and above all, stopping him from serving as a rallying point the whole Khwarezmid troops. Jochi's army was successful in taking over the Khwarezmid center, and repelled numerous contingents of troops who were eager to join with the Shah however it was later found out that there was no reason to fret about Khwarezmid troops forming a mass. While the Khwarezmid force was estimated to be 400,000 however, the Shah was worried that his troops would fall for his if he gathered it all in one location. To be fair to the Shah it was a legitimate concern since his army was comprised of groups of different loyalties. But this would allow for the Mongols to attack the smaller units with greater number of troops and defeat them in a piecemeal fashion.

The Jebe's army was marching to the southwest of the empire while Jochi worked in the northeast region, Genghis moved northwards at the head of the Mongol main army, which included of 50,000 soldiers, and started to take on Otrar throughout the winter 1219-1220. Although the city resisted attempts to breach the walls, Mongols did manage to breach the wall when they found an unlocked gate, which could have been a shady way to open. They then occupied the citadel and held it up for another month, until it eventually collapsed. Inalchuq Governor Inalchuq, who led the conflict in the first instance and was captured while throwing tiles of the roof to the invading Mongols and later executed pouring molten gold down his throat. The city was destroyed by the Mongols, and Genghis himself directing the slaughter and the enslavement of a large portion of the city's inhabitants.

Genghis showed his brilliance when he marched his troops onwards from Otrar and enclosing them in the vastness and obscurity of the Kyzil Kum desert that was believed by the Khwarezmids believed to be completely impervious to any force that was of a reasonable size. But, after enduring inconceivable suffering and shifting from oasis to oasis Genghis Khan managed to escape from the desert just within reach of Bokhara, the main capital city Bokhara. The garrison was unprepared and snared by a brilliant surprise attack. After only three days of besiege they tried to sally, but were killed in the open fields. Genghis later took control of the city and much of which was destroyed to the ground. He then declared, "I am the flail of God, sent to punish you for your sins". Genghis recruited young men to his Mongol army, killed all that remained of the garrison. He also sent anyone who was a skilled craftsman and married females as slaves to Mongolia and then executed the remainder.

Genghis then shifted his troops toward Samarkand which was the capital city of Khwarezm and arrived at the time of 1220. It was enough for his troops to be quickly bolstered by the forces that were from Chagatai and Ogadai and then he laid siege to Samarkand's city. In spite of his formidable Chinese expert in siege, Genghis was facing an army of 100,000 troops at peace behind massive walls brimming with catapults. But Genghis was not likely to be a shrewd or cruel. The Khwarezmids have provoked the Great Khan's anger as they reminisced about how they insulted him. Genghis began an assault on the city, using civilians captured for human shields. after a short period of battle with the garrison that could have surpassed the advancing Mongols were enraged enough to join forces in an attempt to counterattack. Genghis attempted to hide his retreat in order to bring over 50,000 soldiers from the city when they had left the city walls, Genghis turned his army in the opposite direction and massacred the Mongols. About 50,000 soldiers in the garrison died, and a couple of days later, the majority of the remaining soldiers, perhaps more than 40,000 gave up their arms in surrender to Genghis Khan. Genghis Khan then seized the garrison. Mongols later pushed through the city, and sacked the citadel. Then, he renounced his previous promises for those who surrendered and executed all that had taken weapons against his side. Then there was more. Genghis marched the whole civil population of the city, and then killed them until the very last woman, man and child. It was a slaughter of tens, if not hundreds of thousands. The Mongols completed the massacre with the construction of a huge pyramid constructed of skulls of the dead.

Ala-ud-Din was a man who tried to assist the rescue of the city, but had been abducted by Jochi's army He was so frightened that he ran for his life and was surrounded by the forces of Subotai as well as Jebe. The Shah was able to escape on an isolated island on the Caspian Sea with a handful of soldiers loyal to him and Jalal-adDin, his son. was buried (according the old accounts that he died of a broken heart) around 1220.

Genghis However, he was not satisfied. His army marched towards Urgench the second vast well-off trading town that was run by the mother of the Shah. The city was ablaze as Mongol army swarmed, but she was ultimately detained and taken as a prisoner in Mongolia and Genghis's troops occupied the city. The city was soon occupied by the forces of Jochi, Ogadai and Chagatai and the siege was complicated as the city was completely surrounded by marsh and water and made siege work difficult to build. When Genghis and his troops managed to breach the wall but the garrison remained against Genghis, battling house by home and street after street in a gruelling fight in the gutter that hampered the abilities of the quick-hitting steppe horsemen, and made them fight hand-to-hand within narrow, barricaded streets. The losses were heavy for both sides but was a second time that it resulted in the inevitable victory of Genghis. There was a dispute among Jochi whom had been given the city's riches in exchange for his loyalty, and Chagatai whom he believed Jochi had been too gentle about Urgench due to the fear that the city would be destroyed by his portion of the wealth should it be affected too severely, culminated in Genghis giving his city over to Ogadai. This would cause a long-lasting discord between him and Jochi which was made worse by the fact that Jochi's parentage was not clear even though the Khan recognized the latter as his personal.

Medieval representation of Ogadai

Genghis Khan was already showing his brutal side in the wars, however, his capture of Urgench was known for its massive massacre. All the inhabitants of Urgench with the exception of nubile ladies and skilled craftsmen, were taken to be killed and the one Middle Eastern scholar claiming that each out of the nearly 50,000 men that were in Genghis's army had the task of killing 24 individuals. If that is the case, there is a sum of over a million people dead however if exaggerated is likely to mean that the devastation of Urgench was among the bloodiest and most brutal massacres that have occurred in human the history of. The Mongols were able to wreck Khwarezm in the region, decimating whole regions and razing entire cities to ashes, directing rivers to flood them, or burning them in the process of destroying huge stretches of land for farming, and redirecting a river in order to ruin the place of birth for Ala-addin. The goal was the destruction of an entire kingdom.

As Genghis as well as the major Mongol army were involved in these calamities, Genghis also sent a 50,000-strong force under the leadership of his son Tolui to the Khorasan region. It was in the Khwarezmid heartland that was home to numerous fortresses and garrisons. Tolui's forces comprised of a smaller quantity of Mongol soldiers. It was mainly comprised of foreign troops as well as a massive siege machine specifically designed to slash cities of war into dust, and was capable of doing this. Termez and Balkh rapidly fell to Tolui's troops prior to their march on the huge and populated city of Merv which was known as known as the "jewel of Khorasan", with a tiny amount of troops it had was extremely prosperous. Although initially they faced a lot of protests, the garrison in Merv was willing to surrender after Tolui assured them that Merv would not be harmed should they surrender. The pattern outlined by Genghis revealed that this was just an elaborate ruse. Tolui did not keep his word and killed everyone inside the walls, taking the lives of the estimated millions of civilians.

Then, Tolui moved and moved on to Nishapur and Nishapur, which suffered the misfortune to be the place in which Tokuchar the son-in-law of Genghis died as he led an offensive during the battle. Tolui was so angry that He ordered the execution of each living thing in the Nishapur's wall that included cats, dogs as well as other creatures, all with the widow of Tokuchar watching. Then he marched to

Herat however, upon witnessing Nishapur's demise, the residents surrendered without fighting and escaped. Tolui was then responsible for smashing Bamian, Tush and Mashad as well as, 1221 later, by giving Khorasan an empty and degraded Husky, he joined Genghis's army.

In the midst of how Mongolians destroyed the empire, Jalal-add-Din was taking on the throne of his father, left for the mountainous regions of Afghanistan in the mountains of Afghanistan, gathering remnants of Khwarezmid forces to battle Genghis and his advancing Mongols. But Genghis did not want to engage in battle with Jalal-addin and instead drafted an army led by Shihihutag but only to see it destroyed in 1221 close to Parwan by Jalal-adDin. Genghis in a anger over the incompetence of Shihihutag and incompetence, swung into Afghanistan by himself and defeated Jalal-ad-Din's army on the Indus River. He forced his departure to India.

Illustration of Genghis Khan looking over while Jalal Ad-Din is preparing to ford the

Indus

In the end, the Khwarezmid Empire was devastated and destroyed by unimaginable brutality. The Chinese were already able to testify to the potential violence of Genghis Khan, however the Khwarezmids showed the worst of him the result of their leader's pride. The devastation of the country was extremely violent even if you consider Mongol standards. However, it's worth mentioning that the cities that refused to surrender prior to surrender were destroyed while Heart recognized the signs on the wall and was not spared).

Genghis came back to Mongolia however, his victories did not end there. in the west, further territories and bizarre enemies would be waiting for Genghis. In addition, the current campaign also planted the seeds of a raging conflict that could threaten Genghis's power once he was no longer. Following the death of Urgench, Genghis officially named Ogadai the successor to his position, which angered Jochi and forced Genghis to lead his followers to the far reaches in Northern Mongolia and refuse to respond to his father's ever-more angry demand. In the meantime, Genghis had other problems to keep his focus off of his reckless children. There was a rumbling of rebellion within regions like the Jin as well as Xi Xia regions, signaling that China was preparing to explode into a war of all-out. The Mongol army would have to take on combat.

Genghis's Last Campaign

The time was right to head to home, but Genghis Khan decided that his troops was going to march across Afghanistan and into the northernmost portion of India before returning to Mongolia and allow the army to take over previously untouched territories and collect additional plunder. Even though reports suggested that Jin or Xi Xia were provoking each other, Genghis was persuaded to split his army on the advice by Jebe and Subotai, two of his strongest and most capable generals. They suggested the dispatch of a team with 20,000 horses towards the west, and then travel a different route to return back home. Subotai and Jebe as the leaders of their 20,000 troops took off through Persia as well as into contemporary Azerbaijan in the process of sacking Zanjan, Qazvin and Rey and stealing Hamadan and a smart decision to open its gates to Mongols and avoided the bloodshed. Ozbeg was the king of Azerbaijan was able to keep Tabriz which was his capital city and also the undamaged areas of his estates through offering Subotai and Jebe an enormous bribe which included huge amounts of new horses, which was something that the Mongols valued above all other bribes. Jebe and Subotai departed with their army growing to thousands as Kurd as well as Turcoman soldiers, as well as nomad horses archers similar to the Mongols were joined by the prospect of plunder and excitement.

Subotai and Jebe followed by turning east and north to join Subotai and Jebe then shifted north and west into the Kingdom of Georgia, where their vanguard was heavily wounded in the face of an army of 10,000 soldiers led by King George IV in the vicinity of Tbilisi However, in the course of a second battle they managed to destroy the Georgian army, and removing out of the battlefield. Jebe and Subotai were forced to withdraw from Georgia and turned their focus towards the towns that were Maghareh and Hamadan and Hamadan, who did not surrender peacefully and was later destroyed because of their resoluteness.

Chapter 4: A fresco of George IV at Georgia's Betania Abbey in Georgia

The autumn of 1221 In the autumn of 1221 Mongol army retreated into Georgia once more, and even though George IV tried to contest their advance by deploying the help of his army of 60,000 soldiers however, he fell victim to Genghis Khan's traditional strategy of pretending to retreat, after which he savaged his enemies. George IV's troops were totally destroyed and he suffered an injury during the battle. The majority of Georgia was devastated by the Mongols following George IV was defeated, however Jebe and Subotai weren't content with their victory. A bold move, they led their armies through the Caucasus through the middle of winter. Even though the rough terrain cost many lives and the bulk of their siege trains but it proved to be very successful. But the news of their arrival must be able to reach the population as Jebe and

Subotai's troops of approximately 30,000 soldiers they were greeted by a large group consisting comprised of Alans, Cherkeks, Lezgians Khazars Bulgars and Cumans. It was an army that was nearly double that they Mongols were able to gather. But, Jebe and Subotai succeeded in convincing the Cumans to disarm and destroyed the rest of the troops of the coalition. They blundering once more on their pledges; when triumphant, they swiftly cut the Cuman host in pieces and took over one of their most important towns, Astrakhan. The remaining Cuman force fled north together with Mongols following them as Jebe and Subotai waited for the occasion to sit down with the Venetian group and join an alliance that saw them take out any and all forces (chiefly Genoese) hostile to Venetian interest within their territory in the Crimean peninsula.

The Mongols continued to advance into contemporary Russia and were confronted by a hurriedly assembled army made up of different contingents that came from principalities like Kiev and Rus and backed by remaining Cuman army, eager to take revenge. The Russians were seduced by Subotai as well as Jebe into a nine-day frenzied pursuit which was the result of an euphemism to retreat. When they had been thoroughly disorganized, they were repelled by Mongols were able to turn around and destroy the Russians. Their commander, Mstislav the Bold of Kiev stood firm along with his remaining troops in his fortified camps for many days before being ultimately forced to give up his position in exchange for the safety of his troops. However, in the end, Jebe and Subotai ignored their commitments, and executed the honorable (bloodless) execution by slamming him along with his affluent nobles beneath their apron in a celebration banquet.

Twenty-five years following, a papal legate travelling through the countryside, a papal legate took note of the destruction "They attacked Rus, where they made great havoc, destroying cities and fortresses and slaughtering men; and they laid siege to Kiev, the capital of Rus; after they had besieged the city for a long time, they took it and put the inhabitants to death. When we were journeying through that land we came across countless skulls and bones of dead men lying about on the ground. Kiev had been a large and heavily populated town, but now it has been reduced almost to nothing, for there are at the present time scarce two hundred houses there and the inhabitants are kept in complete slavery."

The Millennium of Russia Monument depicting Mstislav (left) as well as his son-in-law Daniel from Galicia

In the wake of Kievan Rus accessible to the Mongols and the city now open to them, the Mongols took over a large portion of the region around until they retreated to the east in 1223. The Mongols also were defeated in a major way in the hands of the Volga Bulgars that during 1223, managed to frighten the local population, either an Mongol group or Mongol vanguard that numbered around 15,000 soldiers, and employ their own strategies to defeat them by tricking the Mongols into pursuit by using an untrue retreat, before launching an attack on the group. Many were killed, and about four thousand were imprisoned during the first major loss for an entire Mongol army in battle. In the battle, Volga Bulgars, as per an ancient chronicler, showed extraordinary business acumen when they ransom the 4000 Mongol prisoners for 4,000 heads of cattle. This ultimately assisted Subotai as well as Jebe. This defeat did not affect the fact that it was a remarkable feat their cavalry assault of three years travelled nearly 9,000 miles and struck the combined armies of nearly dozen nations, and brought Azerbaijan, Georgia, Armenia and Kievan Rus into the Mongol orbit, and delivering huge amounts of gold and silver. Genghis Khan was able to be satisfied by the performance of his troops.

Genghis's troops, who was fighting strong resistance throughout its journey back to Mongol core, was tired as were the soldiers of Jebe and Subotai, who later joined Genghis's troops on the steppes were also exhausted. There was an end to the battle, as Genghis's Tangut Emperor from Xi Xia, despite being the vassal of

Genghis and his army, was fighting for his life and been allied with Jin as a means to win back his their independence. Invigorated by the levies of younger soldiers eager to be part of their elders' glory and glory, in 1226 Genghis was able to take on Jin as well as Xi Xia once again. 1226 also marked the year when Jochi who was still separated of his parents, perished with a mysterious and atypical cause which led some experts to believe that he had been poisoned by Genghis's order as he was unable to answer an official request and therefore was rebelling his own self. In the event that Genghis felt sorrow, he could not display it.

Genghis then pushed his army in Xi Xia, smashing the cities of Ganzhou, Shuzou, Heisui and Xiliang Fu. He also smashed an entire Tangut army that was sent to fight Genghis near Helanshan. Genghis then occupied Lingzhou along Lingzhou's Yellow River and annihilated a Tangut relief army who were sent to help Lingzhou from. His men the next year captured the new Tangut capital city, Ning Hia, and then devastated vast expanses of territory held by the enemy. The Tangut emperor forced the surrender of some provinces of the Tangut center, and then his relentless progress convinced the Tangut Emperor to file a lawsuit for peace in the hope that Genghis will show some leniency. He didn't, and the entire royal family was executed and their dynasty wiped out.

In the latter half of 1227, following the demise of the Tangut Dynasty Genghis Khan himself passed away. The cause of his death remains a source of mysteries and beset by controversy however, a variety of popular theories have been proposed. A fable from the past claimed that an Tangut princess who Genghis received as a wedding gift or had plans at slaying took out a knife that she kept hidden and cut Genghis in his leg or groin, which led to his death due to the loss of blood or the gangrene. It was later reported that the princess to have plunged herself into the Yellow River afterwards to preserve her good character. The demeaning and humiliating death of the princess may be fiction that was the result of the negative propaganda of antagonistic chroniclers following Genghis's demise.

Another more plausible account suggests that Genghis was killed during an ultimate battle with the Tanguts or fell from a horse in a battle or when hunting which aggravated his previous wounds, and then ended his life. Many believe that he died from an illness that was debilitating like tuberculosis or pneumonia, that ended up killing the old Khan off. The fact that by this time Genghis stood in the late sixtys and in constant battle throughout the last fifty years. It seems likely that the years of fighting will have taken its cost, and made even minor injuries or illnesses likely to be fatal.

In the wake of Genghis Khan's demise His body was transported towards the east of the Mongolian heartland. There, according to his wishes, he was buried close to his home in a secret, undisclosed place, as per Mongolian tradition. The funeral guards killed everyone they came across on their journey to the site of his burial to ensure that no one could be able to determine where the bones of Genghis Khan were buried, and then the horses were repeatedly stamped across the site to provide no clues as to the location where Genghis Khan was laid to rest. A few versions of this tale also suggest that a river was diverted to the location.

After his demise Genghis's children enacted the rules laid out in the will he thought of meticulously that followed the battle to defeat the Khwarezmid Empire. Genghis's Mongol army, with more than 130,000 soldiers, was divided between his relatives and the majority (around 100,000 people) being given to Tolui being the youngest with the remainder of 30,000 fell to his male kids (who each had large forces on their own). Genghis's empire also was split into two, but it was as a Mongol empire, with close families and culture ties as per his wish. Ogadai was his most beloved son was awarded his title as Great Khan and the Empire of the Great Khan, comprising most of Eastern Asia and China; Tolui, his eldest son one, got the Mongolian Heartland Genghis's grandchildren Batu and Orda Jochi's sons were given the western Eurasian areas, as well as Eastern Rus as well as Chagatai received Central Asia and Khwarezm. They all built on Genghis's legacy by utilizing the Yassa rule of law as well as the military and administrative infrastructure he had crafted to extend his territory beyond what they had previously been stretched before. Around 1279, or fifty years after the death of Genghis his empire that he created and constructed by hand stretched across Poland up to Korea.

Under Ogedei under Ogedei, the massive empire, that extended from the Mongolian centerlands as well as central Asia up to the Caspian Sea, extended even more to Khwarazmian Persia and the Russian steppes. The 1240s were the time when Mongol horsemen were crossing across the Danube and also the grand principality of Novgorod was submitting to Mongols. Mongols as their lords. On the 9th of August, 1241 the Mongol band of thousands of archers from horses met with a comparable quantity of Polish and

Moravian knights in Liegnitz (Modern Legnica, southwestern Poland). It was the result of an unbeatable Mongol victory.

The Hungarians had been defeated during the Battle of Mohi four months prior in the Battle of Mohi, and the Mongols appeared to be ready to attack Germany as well as Italy however, ultimately they did not. The 1241 Christmas season began, and the Great Khan passed away and the first rulers of the empire travelled to the capital of the empire, Karakorum, to elect the successor to his office. One of them was Batu who was a grandchild of Genghis Khan, through the first son of his Jochi. Genghis gave to him the responsibility for central Asia and also the Russian steppes that he administered under the name Khan. He was being subordinate to the Great Khan of Karakorum. The system he was governed by came to be known as"The Golden Horde, and in Mongolian,

Altan Ord. The English term "horde" invokes a colorful depiction of fierce warriors, however the Mongolian word"horde" refers to the word "camp" or palace. "Golden" may refer to the color gold of Mongols tents or the actual tent that was used by Batu. Also, it is likely it is possible that "Golden" is a transliteration of the Mongolian term for yellow it could also mean "center," in which it is possible that Golden Horde was a reference to "Central Camp."[2The area of Batu is also called Kipchak Khanate (after the Turkic peoples, who were also referred to as Cumans, who resided in central Asia) as well as the Ulus (Realm) in Jochi.

An early Chinese portrayal of Batu Khan.

The Golden Horde was broken into two additional hordes. The Blue Horde covered the Russian steppes, and included the territory of those of the Turkish Cumans (Kipchaks) and also the Bulgars who were settled on the Volga region, as well as the domain of Iran Alans located in the Caucasus. The lands of these peoples were directly controlled by Batu. To the east of Volga was the immense Plains in central Asia that were administered by the Batu's twin brother Orda.

In his role as the senior khan Batu set up his court in Sarai located on the Akhtuba River, a tributary of the Volga approximately 130 kilometers north of the Volga Delta that flows to the Caspian Sea. The main players were Batu as well as Orda who commanded armies across Russia and throughout Eastern Europe. Actually, Batu was invading Austria when news of the Ogedei's demise reached him.

The princes landed in Karakorum and discovered that the administration was controlled by Ogedei's widow Khatun Toregene. She had been plotting to secure the throne of the son of her husband

Guyuk. But the late Great Khan was determined to have the grandson of his Siremum (his child by a different spouse) to be the heir, even though the great princes had confirmed her to the regency but they could not come to an agreement on the succession. Toregene pleaded with Batu to help him, but the latter stayed at Sarai but pleaded for the inability of leaving due to the gout. In reality, Toregene was not interested in his son to take over the throne partly because Guyuk along with Guyuk were at odds over the strategies within Eastern Europe. Guyuk had publicly criticized Batu who could have been branded a traitor and humiliated in a similarly publicly by his father, had the great Khan passed away prior to him being able to do so. However, Guyuk blamed Batu for the loss of his status in the imperial family. Therefore, it was it was in the interest of Batu to hold off his election for as long possible, and by the way, he was increasing the power of his own Golden Horde under his leadership. Toregene an accomplished administrator and politician on her own was also able to make use of this delay to strengthen her position for her son, and also to influence others Mongol princes to vote for him.

If the kurultai was able to not be delayed any longer, Batu did not come personally, but sent envoys possibly fearing that an elected Guyuk could take him out of his post. If this was the case, he should not have been worried since, even though Guyuk was chosen by the majority of Princes of 1246 in the year 1246, the prince was insufficiently powerful to take action against his foes. His mother was not willing to give up her authority, so when she passed away, he felt forced to dismiss her ill-liked ministers, and replace them the trusted servicemen of his father.

Guyuk was a able to be a ruler, yet he was unsure of his position. He was cautious of Batu who was imposing authority on the Russian princes based on the basis of his own authority. Guyuk might have felt threatened when he heard that Batu has approved the Grand Prince Yaroslav II of Vladimir as the suzerain of all other Russian princes. When Batu declared David VI as the new King from Georgia, Guyuk pointedly gave the crown to his opponent. In addition, he started reversing the majority of the government appointments made by Batu.

Chapter 5: The medieval painting of Guyuk

Guyuk was determined to bring the battle with Batu to an end and summoned the Khan of Golden Horde. Batu accepted and marched towards Karakorum and was accompanied by a massive army. In the midst of doubting whether Batu intended to oust him, Guyuk marched westward to be with him. However, Guyuk died in the process on the 20th of April 1248 aged 42.

Batu was, at 43 an elder Mongol prince, and had been the ruler of his Golden Horde for 21 years. Batu used his position to call a kurultai meeting in his territory, and they presented him with the crown. He resigned the crown, but he did not deny the honor. Perhaps he was satisfied to be a part of his position in the Golden Horde and simply wished to make sure that his ancestors of Ogedei which he was not fond of were not ruling. Perhaps He realized he'd not be able to control his entire empire, given the differences between his part of the family and the Jochians as well as the Toluids and the descendants of Genghis's son, Tolui who were represented in the kurultai by Mongke, the prince of Mongke as well as the Ogedeians.

Batu's preferred choice for Great Khan came from Mongke as well, and Batu was elected by a different the kurultai. This time it was at Kodoe Aral in Mongolia but nonetheless under Batu's tutelage. Batu's choice could have been designed to trigger an unrest, which will have made it easier for him to consolidate his influence over the Golden Horde. If it was, the war succeeded in the end, when the Ogedeians as well as other factions of the imperial house fought against Mongke and fell. It was the Golden Horde supported Mongke, and Batu was later named viceroy for the west empire.

Mongke continued to conquer western and northern China as well as expanding to Mesopotamia, Asia Minor, Tibet as well as Korea. At the time that the death of the Khan in 1259 Batu was dead for 4 years earlier. His brief reign was succeeded as the Khan of Golden Horde by his son Sartak (d. 1257) but was succeeded by his sister (or the son), Ulagchi, who lived less than one year. Berke was a son of Batu came next his father, and distinguished himself against other princes from the Golden Horde in being a Muslim. The ancient worship practiced by the Mongols is Shamanist and was generally open to other faiths. Islam was, on the contrary however, was not as at peace and was spread predominantly at the point an axe.

Berke's first contact with the beliefs of Mohammed took place in Sarai in the city of Sarai, where he met with Muslim traders in the Central Asian city Bukhara. As a Khan He set out to create an Islamic government, requiring all in his Blue Horde (over which Batu's descendants Batu enjoyed direct control) to adopt the new religion. The zeal of Berke would lead him into contention with a new Great Khan Kublai (r.1260-1294) who was at war with Kublai's friend, Halagu, Khan of Persia in the aftermath of the siege of Baghdad in 1258.

Kublai's Upbringing

Kublai is one the four sons of Tolui together with his first wife, Sorkhotani, and the brothers, including Monke, Hulagu, and Ariq Boke had all been historically significant. Monke went on to become the Great Khan, and Hulagu was the conqueror of Persia as well as Western Asia and the founder of the Ilkhanids in Persia. Ariq Boke would fight Kublai during a civil war to determine who was the true Great Khan (Szczepanski, 2019).

When he was a teenager Kublai's very first experiences as a government official was when he was given the power to govern a population of 10,000 within Hopei which is a province located in the northern part of China that was centered around what's now the capital city of Beijing. It initially was not a success due to the fact that Kublai didn't supervise his officials properly which led to poor administration as well as corruption which alienated poor. As Kublai and his advisers began to recognize how severe the situation was the issue was solved through the removal of venal Mongolians as well as other officials and substituting them with more ethical officials ("Kublai," 2015). Kublai learned a lesson that Kublai would remember in deciding the best way to fill vacant positions for the future.

In 1251, after Kublai's elder brother, Mongke, became Great Khan He named Kublai as his viceroy, entrusted with the administration of the entire northern region of China. In 1251, it was during this time when Kublai directed advisors to pick the location for a northerly capital city. China and it was named Chengdu, the city. Chengdu. Chengdu was also known as Chengtu and is the origin of the term Xanadu which was later used in European writing. As the viceroy of the northern part of China, Kublai was responsible to overseeing the lives of millions as well as holding significant influence (Szczepanski 2019,).

Mongke

Mongke has reportedly become somewhat sceptical of Kublai's rising influence, so he dispatched two of his associates to look into the matter. They discovered some irregularities (as they likely were ordered to) however, both brothers agreed to peace. There was no doubt that Mongke was the one who gave the order and Kublai was a follower ("Kublai," 2015).

Kublai used to speak Mongolian However, he was never able to communicate in Chinese properly. The primary language used by his administration was Mongolian and many officials were also fluent in the Chinese dialect. Naturally, the fact that Kublai could not communicate in Chinese may be an issue to a man who had the privilege to rule more than 100 million Chinese people.

At the age of a child, Kublai was openminded about religious beliefs. His mother was an Nestorian Christian He was heavily influenced by Haiyun the Buddhist monk who later became Kublai's close advisor and friend. In the meantime, the most customary Mongolian faith was Tengrism it was a kind of shamanistic belief in Tengri, the god of the sky. Tengri. Kublai was believed to have been a follower in a variant that was a part of Tibetan Buddhism ("Kublai," 2015).

China

In contrast to today's unification of China In the time of Mongolian expansion during the 1200s, China was divided into various kingdoms and empires. The divisions of this kind have occurred frequently throughout the long history of China, and the dynasties who managed to unify China frequently split into rival kingdoms. Natural disasters that are unpredictable could reduce the strength of a dynasty, which could result in rebellion. Famines, epidemics, flooding that is devastating, earthquakes and devastating typhoons are all common frequently across the course of China's history. The rulers built granaries for storing rice in the event that a crop was not able to be harvested as well as the Grand Canal allowed massive amounts of food products to move north, though it didn't always stop famines. The 1200s saw plagues and famines were estimated to have killed of more than 35 million people. Moreover, between 1333 and 1337, a long-lasting food shortage claimed the lives of 6,000,000. Many catastrophes could strike simultaneously and weaken a dynasty. ("Kublai Khan"" 2019,).

Furthermore, the dispersed parts of China frequently fought the other parts, and at times nomads from the west and north gained dominance over vast areas of China. China's fate was to have been in this dispersed state when the Mongols gained unity and established their kingdom. The Southern Song dynasty still ruled large portions of China and the two competing empires that ruled China at the time of the period of 13th century had greater in terms of population density than Mongolian domains apart from the Ilkhanids of Persia and Western Asia. China had adopted the early ripening rice which led to an increase in production, while the total Chinese population increased by more than a quarter during the 11th and 10th centuries. In the Northern Song had perhaps 50 million inhabitants, though there could have been as high as around 200 million living in northern China in the last century alone. of Yuan rule and before the start of the Ming one century after. ("Song," 2022).

A large portion of what is today northwestern China was the middle-sized empire of Xi Xia, sometimes also known as Hsi Hsia. Hsi Hsia (1038-1227), which was ruled by the Tangut people. The Tanguts were at first a seminomadic group of people from Tibet similar to the more recent Manchus. The Tanguts built an empire which included various steppes that were nomadic as well as some agriculture-based regions of China. Tanguts had been heavily sinicized after dominating a region of China for more than 200 years.

A large portion of north and northeast China and even Manchuria formed that of the Jin Empire (1125-1234), that was led by the Jurchen Dynasty. They were not Han Chinese - having come from Manchuria located in the northeast but they had a connection to the Manchus who later would be able to conquer the entirety of China until 1644. They were part of the Jin Empire. Jin Empire also incorporated the steppes of northern China, with nomadic communities along with large areas of agricultural land within China ("Song Engagement" 2022).

A little earlier, some time ago, the Khitan people, a different nomadic population who lived on the fringes of China located in Mongolia and Manchuria formed the massive Liao Empire (907-1125) located in northeast China. The Khitan Liao state was destroyed in 1125, thanks to an alliance between both the Jurchens and Northern Song. Following the defeat of the Liao state The Jurchens quickly began to attack their rivals in the Northern Song, drove them from China to the north from the Yangtze River, and hugely increased their power.

Following the Jin changed their views on his Northern Song in 1127, the Song were wiped out of all their territories north of the Yangtze River, including the capital city. But, one from the family of royals managed to escape and declared himself to be Emperor Gaozong (r. 1127-1162) The Song Empire reconstituted itself in the huge Song areas to the south of Yangtze and reorganized into the Empire known as"The Southern Song, which lasted between 1127 and the time of the Mongol conquer ("Song," 2022).

Southern Song Southern Song offered the stiffest and longest-lasting rebuke against the Mongols who depended upon cavalry. The maintenance of cavalry units needed an enormous number of horses. In the heavily settled China the country had little room for horses to graze there was no demand for a horse-intensive, nomadic existence as well as no requirement for horses to be used as draft animals. In China the horses were usually shipped from the north or northwestern regions. Therefore, Chinese power was mostly composed of soldiers. There were two Xias and the Jin. Xia along with the Jin were both cavalry however, the majority of their troops were in the infantry. Southern Song Southern Song, who never was able to boast the powerful, heavy cavalry as the

Jurchens and Mongols they defended themselves using solid fortresses, naval strength and strong defenses along the Yangtze.

Invading the southern part of China was a challenge for the Mongols due to the fact that a large portion of the area was specifically suitable for cavalry while the larger cities served as fortresses. In the meantime they also mastered siege tactics. Chinese were experts in siege warfare and used siege artillery including catapults. As a result, when Mongols were conducting siege warfare and siege operations, their troops were typically Chinese. Chinese specialists in siege operations accompanied Mongolian troops in the west and were utilized to take on cities.

The less powerful empires were wiped out and it took years. Genghis lowered Xi Xia to the status of a vassal in 1210 and the troops from Xia assisted the Mongols in the war against the Jin. In 1227, when the Mongol troops retreated to the west in order to fight Kwarizm as well as other foes within Central Asia, the Xi Xia protested. The Mongols finally defeated them in 1227. The Mongols were furious in their revenge. The conflict with the more powerful and stronger Jin Empire went on for longer in the period 1211-1234 ("Kublai," 2019).

The Mongols were able to accumulate a large number of soldiers, however their method of war wasn't just to crush adversaries to defeat them with the sheer number. They often turned to intimidation, bribery and even terror in order to win. The story of Genghis shows the Mongols for their cleverness at war however the tale itself might be mythological. Genghis faced a resolute protests from Xia city and offered to end the siege if the city provided Genghis with 1,000 cats and 10,000 swifts. He did. The Mongols allowed all of them go free with a piece of burning wool. The Mongols fled back to their cities, which also burned to the ground (Johnson 2021).

In the year 202, when the Mongols started their war against their neighbors in the Jin Empire, they attacked the Great Wall, but that was an act of deceit. As Jin soldiers were Jin troops were protecting their position on the Great Wall, the Mongols moved around the wall's far-end they appeared from the nearby wilderness, and began to attack from the west as the Jin troops were focused on attacking the Great Wall itself (Johnson, 2021).

The Song were allies to the Mongols at the end of their time of the battle against Jin and perhaps didn't realize they Mongols represented a bigger threat. In the course of the siege on the Jin Kaifeng city Kaifeng with perhaps 1 million residents The huge Song army took part as a complete member, using the siege engines and a swarm of soldiers to attack the walls and playing crucial in winning the war just as the Mongols. Following the Jin surrendered in 1235 Song made a move to capture various Jin cities that they believed were theirs in exchange for joining the Mongols. The Mongols were double-crossed by the Song they then pursued the Song army, beat them down, then pushed back to the Yangtze (Johnson 2021).

Another non-Chinese state situated in the extreme southwest of Yunnan that was called the Kingdom of Dali (also called the Kingdom of Nanzhao). To the south of it was Vietnam (which didn't include the southern part of Vietnam in the past) as well as Burma. The to the west Dali there was Tibet. Dali wasn't Chinese however was greatly in the influence of Chinese tradition.

The battle against the Song continued during the reign of Mongke Khan. The year 1252 was the time Mongke directed Kublai to take on the Dali kingdom of Yunnan located in China's southwest. This would open an opportunity to attack Song through the southwest, as well as the west, through Tibet. In the past it was believed that the Dali kingdom was a stable place for centuries with a tense relation to China as well as Tibet.

Kublai took the majority of the year prepping for his invasion. it was an arduous battle however, the Dali kingdom's ruling class gave up and accepted Mongol rule in 1256. Mongke named Kublai as his governor for his newly conquered Dali kingdom. This area was to be utilized for the army that were advancing on Song. Dali was expected to provide troops as well as tributes to the battle. Kublai may also have appointed a lot of Dali officials and royals in their former positions after they agreed to take over Mongol as their overlordship. The year 1258 was the time Kublai defeated his rivals in the Song in the Southwest while Mongke struck via the northwest ("Yuan," n.d.).

The fall of Dali kingdom led the Mongols close to the borders of Vietnam as well as Burma. The Mongols fought in a conflict between the two countries in 1257-1258. Vietnam between 1257 and 1258, before the Mongols moved north in order to contend in the Song. The Mongols were in Burma as well as the adjacent territories during the reign of Kublai however the specifics of the events that took place there remain unclear ("Kublai," 2018).

Chapter 6: Geography, Flora and Fauna
GEOGRAPHY

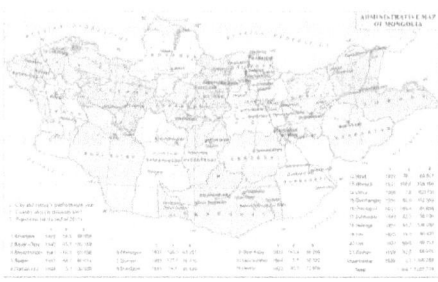

Mongolia's land area Mongolia is situated in the middle of Asia between 41deg35', 52deg 06' in elevation and 87deg47', 119deg of longitude. Mongolia is in close proximity to Russia across 3485 km to the north, and China to the south along 4676.9 kilometers to the south. Mongolia is comprised of 1564.1 thousand square miles of terrain. It extends 2392 kilometers from the west to the eastern frontier and 1259 kilometers from north towards the southern frontier.

Mongolia is the 18th biggest country on earth by area and split by administrative division into 21 provinces (aymag) as well as capital city. Aymags are subdivided into 330 provinces (sum) as well as capital city Ulaanbaatar is split into nine districts.

Administrative map of Mongolia

The average altitude is 1580 meters over sea level. The highest point is Huyten (Khuiten) summit (4374 m) in the west. at the bottom is Hoh Nuur (Khokh Lake) depression to the east at 532m higher than sea-level.

Physical map of Mongolia

The mountains and ridges of Mongol Altay and Govi-Altay, the Hovsgol mountainous region, Hangay and Hentey are juxtaposed against vast plains, depressions and valleys. The relief in its entirety is formed during the transition zone that connects mountains in the south of Siberia towards those of the Central Asia plains. Its relief has distinctive aspects of the continent's long expansion. It is awash with the diversity of structural tectonic shapes that are inherited from platforms of the past and orogenic areas then rejuvenated by new orogenic movement. Deflation and erosion processes are well-known. The Neotectonics as well as the seismicity (9-12 Richter's Scale forces) can be seen clearly in reliefs of Mongolia.

Hentey Mountains

Three distinct environments based on their nature are distinct from Mongolia. They include Mongolia's Hangay and Hentey mountains and The Central Asian land of high plains, depressions and mountain ranges and the Great Hyangan mountains. The majority of Mongolia comprises high plains, mountains and depressions. The most distinctive features of Mongolia are additional continental climate as well as endoreic hydrographic basins that have intermittent permafrost, ephemeral water runoff and a lack of forest; steppes that are dry desert steppes, semidesert and desert landscapes dominate. Trans Altay Govi appears to be the most dry area of the country. There are well-known as stony deserts, named Hamada as well as exposures of salt-bearing sediments from Mesozoic as well as Cenozoic. Certain ecosystems of Mongolian deserts have oasis-like areas filled with vegetation and aquifers.

Tsagaan Suvarga of Dundgovi aymag (Desert steppe)

Amazing monuments from Mongolian tradition and history are in the hands of the state and local guardianship. Mongolian laws provide for the protection of ecosystems and nature of the nation. Mongolia's distinctive landscapes, creatures and vegetation are globally recognized. Numerous animals are included in the International Red Book as well as Mongolia's National Red Book. Mongolian National Red Book.

Beautiful Mountain Bogd Han located in the south of Ulaanbaatar became the sanctuary in 1778. was one of the very first national parks in the world.

Mountain Bogd Han

In 1994, in line of "Law on conservation areas with special protection" adopted by Mongolian Parliament, areas which had to be protected by the government were classified in the following manner:

-Sanctuary

-National Park

-Nature Reserve

-Memorial Places

The protection of the wild in this nation has been at the spotlight of the international community and these places were listed as "WORLD HERITAGE" by UNESCO.

As Nature Reserves:

-Uvs Lake Basin

-Govi Great Desert

-Mountain Govi Gurvansayhan

Hovsgol Lake, the homeland of the Shamanic Tsaatan tribe

-Mountain Bogdhan

-Mountain Burhanhaldun

-Mountain Otgontenger

Erdenezuu Monastery (Ovorhangay aymag)

As Historical and Cultural Reserves:

-Ruins of Harhorin

-Erdenezuu

-Tovhon hiyd (monastery)

Balgas from Har

-Monuments of Kultegin and Bilge Khaan

Petroglyph (inscriptions in the rock) from Tsagaan Salaa

The Petroglyph (inscriptions on rock) in the rock of Hoyd Tsenher

Amarbayasgalant Monastery, etc.

The mineral resources of the nation is extensively studied and its geochemical setting is of particular interest. In the course of its evolution, seven tectonic epochs and the six most important endingogenic and magmatic ore-forming phases are identified. In addition, Cenozoic volcanism occurs in a wide range of. The mineral sources include coal, oil and combustible schist; peat; manganese, iron and titanium; chromium and vanadium; copper lead, zinc nickel, arid copper and silver molybdenum, tungsten bismuth; arsenic, bismuth and uranium. Also, oscillator quartz Iceland the spar, fluorite graphite, asbestos mica, magnesium; sulfur, barite, and salts soda, the color stones, phosphorus construction materials, and naturally, ground water minerals, both fresh and mineral as well as thermal.

Map of mineral resources in Mongolia

Mongolia is among the handful of countries in the world which have managed to preserve the unique natural beauty of its. Since the Mongolians have worshipped the ground, the blue sky and mountains and rivers from ancient time, and on opposite, in spite of a the small size of their population, urbanization and industrialization aren't yet advancing rapidly, Mongolian people have preserved the wildness of their homeland.

The last 70 years, in addition to the animal industry, Mongolia has been developing new fields of industry that are based on natural resources and transport, such as mining and processing of minerals and power construction materials, wood processing and production along with agriculture, and this has led to a dramatic change in both socioeconomically and environmental ratio. In addition, with the shift to market economy the urbanization process and industrialization has increased and the percentage of fields that depend on the natural resources of the economic growth. As a result of its use of natural resources, the quantity of them has decreased and the environmental quality has become worse, leading to ecological inequalities.

Climate Mongolia which is a landlocked state situated far away from seas and boasts an extremely cold weather. The cloudiness decreases if you move to the south, and it's a sunny climate. When winter comes around, because cold air moves through from to the North Pole and stays for many days the atmospheric pressure rises and produces anticyclone. This anticyclone's region is particularly concentrated in the lowlands around Uvs Lake and Hyargas Lake. At the middle of the anticyclone, wind power is low and there are times when there's none at all and the more wind current shifts from the center towards east, the more speed of the wind with an increasing atmospheric pressure changes.

Summer (Herlen River)

In Mongolia wind patterns are predominantly to both the north and west at any time of the year. While wind speed is not greater than one meter per second in the lowlands, it typically moves at a rate of between 2 and 5 meters in steppes that are open. The high winds that reach 15 m per second or greater are extremely rare and their frequency increases when you move further towards south. When it is the time of year for strong winds dust storms as well as blizzards can be seen frequently. they may last for up to 1 to 6 hours. In fact, they have had instances that were prolonged to as long as twelve hours. The most windy province is Dundgovi's aymag's middle Mandalgovi where the wind speed could reach up to 40 meters per second. In northern parts of the country, winter can be very cold and long, and the soil freezes 3-4 meters deep. In the south, however, the soil could be frozen 2.5 meters in depth. The average January temperature can be as low as 35degC (-31degF) within the lower lands and is the coldest part of the United

States. In the Uvs Lake Depression, the maximum temperature is less than 50 degC (-58degF). The winter months are warm in the east-central parts of the nation and during July, the average daytime temperature is 25degC (77degF) and the temperature is 40degC (104degF) within govi regions including Dornogovi's Aymag's Central Saynshand.

Normal temperature map of Mongolia

Since the beginning of time, the temperature average has raised by 1.5degC across the entire country as a result the global warming. The ratio of precipitation is different While Mongol Altay Mountain ranges with three thousand meters or more are able to receive 250-300mm annually heavy rainfall, the exact amount falls on zones that sit at 2000m within the Hangay Mountains, 1500 meters in Hovsgol and 1000m or more high in the Hentey

Mountains. The most humid area of Mongolia can be found in the Hentey and Hovsgol mountain ranges. The territory of Mongolia summer rains make 60% to 70% of the the annual average in the range of 200-220 mm.

Winter (Hovsgol Lake)

Wintertime snowfalls cover the nation from October until in the early part of April. The snow cover is thick in the mountains and lasts for an extended period of time, but there isn't permanent snow covering on the Govi and steppe areas. Contrary to other seasons the air in spring is very dry. The average humidity of the air is at 30 percent. In the south, the relative humidity is lower than. In general, under favorable conditions, the humidity levels can be as low as 60% to 70% of the needed normal levels.

Surface water. Over 3800 are permanently flowing rivers within Mongolia. Mongolia. Mongolian rivers are located in Arctic, Pacific and land sealed Central Asian River Basins. It is believed that the Arctic Ocean Basin contains Selenge the most important river in Mongolia. Its Pacific Ocean Basin's design is rather sparse. includes several major rivers like Halhyn Gol, Herlen, Onon and Ulz among others. Zavhan, Tes and several others are part of the areas that are landlocked Central Asian River Basin. Rainfall plays a crucial role in the supply of water to rivers and underground supply of water generally comprises 20%-40% of the total. The proportion decreases as the typical height of water accumulation fields.

Map of Hydrograph

In the central southern, south east and central regions of the country, the The density of river structures is lower than in those in the western and northern mountainous regions. Furthermore, some river flows flow into lowlands, and then disappear.

Tuul River

Pebbly spots are often found in the mountains that surround Govi lowlands in Mongolia and flood during the season of rain, extending many kilometers. Glaciers and peaks with permanent snow cover which are witnessing glacier's time can be observed at Altay, Harhiraa, Turgen, Hangay, Soyon and the other mountains.

Hovsgol Lake

There are around 4000 lakes within Mongolia as well as larger ones situated in the western region as are smaller ones found in the eastern portion of Mongolia. The largest lakes like Hovsgol, Uvs, Hyargas, Har-Us, Har, Boon Tsagaan Orog, Ulaan are divided into running and stagnant according to their chemical composition, they may be identified as freshwater or salt lakes. The largest freshwater lake is Hovsgol and the largest salt lake can be found in Uvs.

Soil There are more than thirty different types of soil that can be found within Mongolian soil. The brown and black types generally occur in mountains in high forests, steppe areas with woods, grey-brown or grayish earth occurs predominantly in deserts steppes and similar to desert areas, and as well as brown earth within steppe zones. Based on the soil field composition that brown earth makes up 46 percent of the soil, while desert-like-steppe grayish earth covers 14 percent of total soil.

Soil map of Mongolia

Lowland, steppe and valley soils comprise a larger portion of the soils of the nation.

Concerning the agrochemical properties of the soils in farmland, amount of compost ranges from 2.3-3.8 percent of soil, and the content of potassium, nitrogen and phosphorus is comparatively low.

FLORA

The Mongolian region is situated at the heart of the East Siberian Central Asiatic extra continental section; this is distinguished by the uniqueness of its plant life and its distinct shift in vegetative connections from north towards the south.

In mountain areas, the differentiating of high altitude forest is evident. The forests are thriving mainly in mountain areas. In Mongolia there are a variety of endemic as well as subendemic species of vegetation can be found. It is possible to see in the piedmonts the range of trees, bushes and blossoms, particularly during spring, when anemone rose, edelweiss and geranium bloom. The steppes and hills are Rhododendron dahuricum Pyrola Incarnata Pulsatilla flavencens Oxvtropis caespitosa, and many more.

Flora, of Monhjargalan (Tov Aymag and Mongonmorit sum)

It is composed of 128 families with 823 genera, and 662 kinds of flowering plants. 39 genera, 133 families as well as 930 lichen species 38 families 162 genera, and four17 species of moss 28 families, 136 genera as well as 875 mushroom species sixty families, 72 genera and 728 algae species; as well as 600 species of microorganisms found in Mongolia. The vegetation can be classified into these zones: alpine zone high forest zone, wooded-steppe zones the steppe zone, semi desert or desert-like steppe zone and the desert zone.

Mountains of Hovsgol

High mountain belt nature of the characteristics of plants Mongolian high mountains are broken down into four subdivisions. The upper part of the mountain there are bare rock with no vegetation other than some lichens that are stuck to the rock surfaces. Higher up higher, there will be less or no vegetation and the only thing that remains is endless snow, bare rock, and a fault line made of rocks. There are a few plants like carex, dryadanthe, kobresia Saxifraga Cemua, Potentilla Gelida, P.biflora are occasionally seen within the hillsides of mountain the peak. A few cold-tolerant plants like dryas, carex, kobresia salix Kobresia sibirica K. Bellardii Ptilagrostis mongholica Poa altaica tend to grow in the plateau of a mountain. The lower part of the mountain ranges between the ridges and peaks do Pinus sibirica and Larix sibirica thrive. The main characteristic of the vegetation in the zone is that most plant species are shrubs, or undershrubs. Mosses such as Aulacomium and other shrubs like Betula Rotundifolia B. Fruticosa, Salix divaricata and the lichens of the Cetraria generally grow within the vegetation belt.

The end of Altay Mountains (Omnogovi aymag)

Shrubs are prevalent in the mountains that rise between the peaks and the ridges of Bulnay, Tarvagatay, Han Hohiy, Hentiy, Hovsgol and Hangay Mountains. But, the vegetation belts of plateau-like summits, and the areas in between peaks and ridges that are covered with the moss and lichen are typically found in Hovsgol, Hentey, Hangay, Mongol Altay, and Govi-Altay Mountains.

Orostachys

Limonium Flexuosum

Wild onion

Although the humidity and precipitation is extremely high, it's the only plants that can withstand cold conditions thrive in the mountainous areas because of the ice layer and perpetual snow. It is also because of the insufficiency of temperature for plant growth extreme cold weather conditions during the entire year and a wide variation in daytime temperatures. Because of the fact that the continental dry climate is evidently affecting the majority of high mountain ranges in the mountainsides of Hangay, Mongol Altay, Govi-Altay Mountains are steppe or desert vegetation grow. are visible on the flat peaks of mountain ranges.

Forest Mongolian high forests spot bordering the southern edges of the Siberian extended range of forested mountains. Mongolian forests are in general mountains that are cultivated on the tops of mountains.

Forest (Hentiy Mountain Range)

In light of the climatic conditions like precipitation fall, primary direction of wind flow as well as the degree of sunlight intensity, there isn't any forest either on the southern or eastern slopes, however generally, they're on the northern part of a mountain.

Density of forest makes up 8.1 percent. According to 1995 data, the total land area of forest in the country is 17516,000 hectares which is 92 percent of it is forest, with only 8 percent being areas that are not wooded. Larch forests are the main source of wood and Siberian pine forests supply 77.2 percent, while pine trees-12.1 percent, the birch 5.3 percent. spruce 4.9 percent, aspen, poplar and fir comprise only 0.1 percent of the wood recourse.

Cedar

Huckleberry

Black Currants

In the Govi region, does saxaul develop as research suggests that the wood resources of saxaul are 1500 thousand square meters.

Mongolian forests are continuously affected through Central Asian desert and steppe drying climate influences.

A lack of regenerative capacity and a highly combustible character as well as timber processing fires are the main causes of decreasing forest cover.

This belt includes subsidiary hills from Hentiy, Hangay, and Mongol Altay Mountains. The most distinctive feature of the belt is its unique relationship between steppe and forests that occur in the mountains. In the steppes of mountain regions grasses are the most common plants to develop and spread out dispersed in line with the soil surface and the land.

Festuca ovina, Poa attenuata, Agropyron cristatum, Bromus inermis Helictotrichon Schellianum; Carex pediformis, Carex duriuscula; Aster alpinus Artemisia frigida Potentilla and Androsace are most often seen in the mountain steppe area.

The vegetation in Mountain Slope (Hentiy Aymag)

Scabiosa

Delphinium

Pedicularis Longiflora

Lily

Lilium silvestre flavum

Stellaria Dichotoma

Corydalis

Bellflower

Linaria Buriatica

Hippophae (Sea Buckthorn)

Russula aeruginea

Russula aurata

Amanita

Suillus

Leccinum

Agaricus cantharellus L.

Steppe Zone Steppe is the place in which dry grassy plants mainly are found. The steppe zone includes Eastern Mongolia, Central Halh plateau, a vast plain, as well as to the west, it narrows as it passes through the slopes that run downhill towards the southern rim of Han Hohiy. The narrow strip runs towards the west, and reaches the lowlands of Ih Nuur (Great Lakes). Stipa capillata, Stipa baicalensis, Stipa Krylovii, Stipa grandis Agropyron the cristatum, as well as Potentilla acaulis are all common in the steppe area.

Lilium Pumilum

Dandelion

Geranium Pratense

Thistle

Echinops Bannaticus

Leontopodium Ochroleucum (Edelweiss)

Adonis Vernalis

Steppe area that resembles desert. This area was formed in the region that borders Central Asian desert and Mongolian steppe. It includes lowlands that are part of the Great Lakes, a valley of the Many Lakes, low-lying height of Dornogovi and Govi-Altay Mountains.

Because of the lack of precipitation and the relative humidity, plants here are more dry and resistant to the draughts of the steppe zone than other species in the steppe zones and consequently to this, many species of plants have developed a habit of keeping water within their leaves.

Plants that belong to this region are Stipa gobica, S. glareosa, Stipa orientalis and numerous others.

Haloxylon (Omnogovi aymag)

Allium Polyrrhizum

The desert zone is a difficult area to grow in, despite the adequate heat source, it's impossible for plants to thrive in the desert since the annual average precipitation of less than 100 millimeters, is not enough to flourish.

Haloxylon Salicornicum (Omnogovi aymag)

There are 497 plant species that have been recorded. Of the all the species, there are 389 of herbaceous species and the 108 species of woody and plant species that are shrubby. Alongside the aforementioned diversifolia, which is a plethora of as well as saxaul, elm and saxa various species of tamarisks may be seen within the area of an oasis.

Interzonal plant life Interzone of plants includes meadow, oasis, a shrubby grassland grove with a river. It also includes an eucalyptus and poplar tree grove as well as a water meadow and the feather-grassy relief. Hygrophytic plants, grassy plant, tussocks and color-coordinated herbs dominate in the plant cover and the plants from every zone and belt apart from High Mountain and high forest belts. They can be viewed in this.

FAUNA

Mongolia is among the oldest centers that spawned sub-aerial species on the planet. Due to its isolation of the world's civilized and the vast, uninhabited territories that was a large number of animals that were kept that were lost from other parts of the globe.

Skeleton of Tarbosaurus (MNHM)

Old endemics and flora relics have a distinctive character. The fauna of Mongolia is diverse and rich There are 630 varieties of vertebral mammals, comprising mammals of 146 species, over 450 species of birds (120 species of which have their economic value in hunter-gatherers and trappers). There are around 8 species of reptiles and amphibians, there are more than 70 varieties of fish. Entomofauna has a wide and varied variety and includes a variety of ecosystems and zones of insects. In this area, one will find uncommon and endangered species of animals like Hulan (Asiatic wild ass), tahi (Przewalskii's wild horse) Govi bear (mazaalay) and the havtgay (wild two-humped camel) (wild two-humped camel), argalis (wild mountain sheep) and snow leopard. jeiran, saiga and bustard beauty (also known as jack), hoof Mongolian Saksaul Jay, Eagle lammergeyer, griffon brown owl, eagle pelican, owl, and the swan (desert and steppe regions) such as deer and elk Siberian Ibex, sable marten, otter, beaver the pheasant, and so on. The rivers also have found salmon species that have been met (taimen and linok), harius and in the sig) and sturgeon, sterlet and others.

Zoological map of Mongolia

Mammals' Mongolian mammal's class includes Asian, Eastern Asian, and Siberian mammals, however the most prominent representatives include Central Asian species. According to their range, mammals could be classified as mountain mammals, forest mammals plain mammals, and desert mammals. 40% of mammals are hibernating during the winter months. Mammals like dhole Otter, govi bear Przewalski's wild horses Mongolian antelope of the saiga, Bactrian camel, bear, the jerboa and kozlov's Pygmy jerboa. long-eared jerboa marbled polecat leopards, wild cats wild ass, wild boar east Siberian moose, Ussurian reindeer, moose goitered gazelle (jeiran) as well as argali have been protected and are registered in "Red Book".

Mongolian Dormouse (Omnogovi aymag, Gurvantes sum)

Eagle (Nalayh district in Ulaanbaatar)

The bird species of the Birds are numerous and the composition of them is different, since the migration routes of birds that originate from the Pacific and Indian Oceans, as well as that of the Mediterranean Sea to the Arctic traverses Mongolia. While 78 percent of Mongolian birds are migrants and 20 percent are residents.

Black Vultures (Ovorhangay aymag, Burd sum)

Around 320 bird species lay eggs and remain in Mongolia in the summer. Around a dozen species of birds fly in from to the Arctic coasts as well as Tundra and spend the winter months in Mongolia. They include the Siberian white crane the white naped, hooded and azure crane hobara bustard the gull, reed's Parrot Bill spoonbill, pelican the black stork, the whooper swan muted swan, swan goose, bar-headed goose, osprey and white-tailed eagle and Himalayan griffon. Ring-necked Pheasant Little Whimbrel is at risk of becoming extinct They are also protected and recorded within the "Red Book".

Swans (Hentiy aymag)

The Pacific Ocean Basin's fisheries and lakes are full of fish. There are more than 40 species of fish, such as the black river sturgeon, taimen as well as hemibarbus, sazan and among others. The Arctic Basin's lakes and rivers have around twenty species of fishes, such as pike, taimen and sturgeon darkhad white fish as well as other species. However, only five species of fish, such as Mongolian grayling as well as Altaic Ostan that live in lakes and rivers that are part of the landlocked Central Asian Basin. The Altaic ostan is a species of fish with remarkable adaptation, can live in a salt lake, or within the river. The fish can even survive in small streams. It is a thriving species. Western Mongolian grayling and the Altaic ostan are both considered to be indigenous of Mongolian waters. The Baikal Sturgeon as well as Hovsgol Omul are both native to Mongolia. Hovsgol Omul are listed within the "Red Book".

Amphibians live in swamps, within ponds, as well as in the lakes of a moist cooler northern area. There are a few species like Siberian salamanders, forest fog, black-spotted the frog, as well as Asiatic grass frogs can be found on marches and lakes in steppes and forests. But, the green toad as well as the Mongolian toad can be found not just in the north, but in the desert lowlands. In the lowlands, both Siberian Salamander and Asiatic grass frog are recorded within the "Red Book".

Reptiles There's 22 reptile species including 13 species of lizards can be classed into three categories and nine snake species are among the four major categories. They are mostly found warmer areas like steppes and desert areas.

Snake (Selenge aymag, Mandal sum)

Insects have the highest number by species, as well as the most researched living thing in the Mongolian category of animals. Certain scholars consider it to be established the fact that within Mongolia there should be between around 22-25 thousand varieties of insects. According to research, over 13000 species as well as 3200 different classes of insect species have been identified to date. Many insects from Central Asia are among the insects that inhabit the United States. The study has revealed that more than 190 species of insects contribute for agriculture. However, there are more than six hundred additional species that threaten both agriculture and our hygiene.

Grasshoppers (Selenge aymag, Mandal sum)

There are numerous species of animal who are in danger of disappearing due to human's directly or indirectly influenced and the adverse impacts of the climate as well as changes in the natural world. Mongolia is paying a lot of interest in the protection of unique species of animals. As per the laws, Mongolia is registered in the "Red Book" and has protected exotic animals, such as the Prwalskii's wild horse, Saiga the tatarica beaver and govi bear (mazaalay) the wild Bactrian camel (havtgay) as well as many more.

Exhibit of Argali as well as Siberian Ibex (yangir) (Natural Museum of History, Dundgovi aymag)

There are more than fifty species of mammals more than 130 species game birds, as well as around 40 fish species which can be hunted to make the most of their skins flesh, meat, horns the musk, and many other organs. They include marmots, Mongolian gazelle, brown bear, fox and wolf smaller flying squirrel wolverine and raccoon dogs, alaschan suslik, among others. Hunting protected game animals like moose, deer wild mountain sheep Asiatic Ibex, and other protected animals is permissible to hunters from abroad and a small number of hunters is regulated by the Federal Government.

Chapter 7: History

ANCIENT PEOPLE

Paleolithic period, which was between 750 and 800 thousand years ago which falls located in the end of the Paleolithic period. These were the people living on the territory of Mongolia. The homesteads and other remains of people were discovered in places of the Saynshand of Dornogovi aymag, the Nariyn river that flows through Olziyt sum, Tsagaan cave of Bayanlig sum, and Bosgo in Shinejinst sum, Bayanhongor aymag as well as the valley of Tsahiurt of Omnogovi Aymag, and also stone arms, which were commonly used by the inhabitants in the time of their discovery, hadn't been discovered in ordure finds as well.

The ancient civilizations (Exhibit at NMM)

In the period 100000-40000 BC during the time of the middle Paleolith There were glaciations and as a consequence, the biggest mountains were covered in the ice, and many species of animals and plants within Mongolia were lost to. Wild mammals, horses, belly rhinos, as well as some species of birds and fish, lived in humid and mild zones along the banks lakes and rivers. Due to the ice-free glaciers and the rapid change in weather, both animals and plants along with human bodies as well as minds were subject to change. Orhon I VII was located within the area of Harhorin amount, Ovorhangay aymag, Argalant I, Orog Lake I, II of Bogd sum, Bayanhongor aymag, Otson Maanit of Hanbogd sum, Omnogovi aymag, Altantsogts, Altantsogts sum, Bayan-Olgiy aymag and the Rock Rashaan settlement Batshireet sum The Hentiy aymag is part of settlements, the ordure and blacksmith's settlements of the time.

In the middle of Paleolithic period, which was the time when people began using fire. It was vital to the development of people as well as, the differences in labor between women and men were more prevalent, namely women, who were in charge of looking after their kids and removing roots of plants as well as seeds, were also required to care for their homes hearths. As the weather changed to cooler temperatures, they started to build stone walls for covering the pits with animal skins and hides, and also to spread herbaceous grasses, dry grasses as well as animal skins to shield themselves from the rain, sun and wind, making use of caves that were formed by natural processes or gorges as well as rocks.

It was believed that around 40000-15000 BC and later in the Paleolithic period, glaciers were beginning to decrease and the current climatic conditions was in place. The climate was becoming dry, and then transformed into a continental climate, which along with the rhinos and mammoths, were the wild horse, cattle Ibexes, deer and wild sheep, saigas white foxes as well as ostriches as per paleontological studies. Bone remains from the animals were discovered in regions of the right bank of Bugant river. Yoroo as well as Ingettolgoy, Selenge aymag, Eg the river basin of Hutag-Ondor sum Bulgan Aymag, Har Yamat and Har Yamaat of Jargalant sum, Tov aymag and also within the vicinity of Ulaanbaatar city. Ovorhangay, Omnogovi, Dornogovi, Suhbaatar and Hovsgol aymags. The tracks of the early stone armaments of the people have been all over the place of our nation. Particularly, numerous settlements, blacksmith and ordure locations have been found within these areas, including Moyltyn am of Harhorin, Ovorhangay Aymag Rashaan was in Batshireet sum Hentiy anamag Ih Bulgan of Olziyt sum, Bayanhongor aymag, Songino mountain and Buyant-Uhaa of Ulaanbaatar city. Tsetserleg town Arhangay aymag Dorolj I, II of Eg river Hutag-Ondor sum Bulgan Aymag, Hovd-14 Bayannuur-13. Manhan-5. Bugat-2 Altay-1 Mongol Altay mountain ranges located in the Bayan-Olgiy as well as Hovd aymags, as well as within the basins of major rivers such as Orhon, Selenge, Tuul, Onon and Herlen.

The Men Stone Map from Mongolia

One of the most significant aspects that are associated with the initial period of more advanced Paleolith are the significant changes that occurred to the human body. In that period, the stone armaments were much more advanced than they are today. As a result the hunting activity had evolved significantly and people were able to reside in some areas for long periods of duration. A good example of this are the Valley Moylt and rock Rashaan settlements that allowed people to stay for an extended time of around 20000 years from the Paleolithic period through Mesolithic period. While digging the area, there was the foundation of many stones, the remains of cutting devices and two-edged knives scrapers, devices to perforate or pierce knives, sharpened and edged objects. Ancient people developed the concept of living, and a certain type of social structure. The first form of co-operative living of society was the matriarchy.

Mesolithic period Mesolithic phase (15000-8000 BC) was a period of transition to earlier Old Stone Age to the New Stone Age.

The transitional period is referred to as"the Middle Stone Age and at this Age in which bows and arrows were utilized in place of spears became a dazzling advancement in the development of armaments and, more importantly, the stony weapons and devices were significantly upgraded. In the same time, aside of hunting, they started to increase fishing opportunities as well as keep wild animals in their homes and cultivate crops. Researchers found and examined the previously unexplored sights of the Mesolithic period in regions of the left bank Herlen River (located at opposite the Choybalsan town), Heree mountain of Halhgol sum, Dornod Aymag, Moyltyn am Ovorhangay aymag Rashaan was of Hentiy Aymag Chihen Aguy (cave) the Bayan-Ondor sum Bayanhongor Aymag Baruun as well as Zuun Hayrhan Mountains of Bulgan sum, Omnogovi aymag and Dulaany govi of Erdene sum Dornogovi aymag and the areas in Dundgovi Bayan-Olgiy Hovd Govi-Altay, Bayan-Olgiy and Suhbaatar Aymags.

The map of the Deer statue of Mongolia

Neolith period In during the Neolith time (8000-3000 BC), the patriarchy was a reality in Mongolia. The tools and equipment for labor had remain the same for all tribe participant. The primary type for arranging the living quarters and animal husbandry was a tribal camping. Utilizing natural-ready products such as hunting animals collecting plant roots and seeds were not a priority but, farming for crops and livestock management that looked towards the Mesolithic time frame more developed.

Experiences, practices and skills in the art of making armour using stone, were more advanced than usual, and a variety of sorts of household goods were created with exquisite and delicate patterns. According to the facts about stone graves, burial objects as well as icons, it suggests that the people of the past were influenced by beliefs. A variety of vases and arms have been found in the ancient human settlements that were located in provinces such as Bayanhongor and Govi-Altay. Dornogovi, Dornod, Dundgovi, Zavhan, Ovorhangay, Omnogovi, Suhbaatar, Tov, Uvs and Hentiy aymags. From them, 12 settlements located along bank of Sagsay River, Bayan-Olgiy aymag, Zuuh of Bayanlig sum, Bayanhongor aymag, Bayanzag of Bulgan sum, Omnogovi aymag, Ustay and Burgastay of Monhhaan sum, Suhbaatar aymag and sightseeing of Tamsagbulag, Dornod aymag can be mentioned.

Stone Amulet (Neolithic age 4000-3000 BC, NMM)

The Neolith period, weapons as well as home appliances were developed and, in addition, copper was employed for manufacture of. People living in Mongolia were in during the Neolith period in the middle of three millennia BC. Copper mines' ruins and excavations have been discovered at Omnogovi, Dornogovi, Dornod, Ovorhangay, Bayanhongor and Tov Aymags. Stone mallets that have a groove in their middles as well as heavy nestles and hammers that were used for digging copper ore in the past and were discovered in locations like Oyu tolgoy, Zelt, Hanbogd sum, Omnogovi aymag. Two small and big stone objects with intricately carvings of heads of wild sheep belonging with those of the Neolithic period were discovered in the region in Manhan sum, Hovd aymag and Hovd aymag. They are unique and intriguing discoveries regarding the time period. Furthermore, rock art featuring unusual images were discovered in the Chuluut River valley of Arhangay province, as well as certain areas of Mongolia.

Bronze as well as Iron Ages the Bronze Age began around 3000 BC and was located in Mongolia. It was a Bronze Age transitive period was an transformation in the cultural and economic spheres as well as fundamental shifts had taken place in social interactions. Remaining evidence of bronze armour produced in a few areas of the country include mining sites, bronze casting ovens as well as moulds for bronze objects. Rectangular graves are an archeological find connected to the Mongolian Bronze armament time period. For the items discovered in these graves most of them are tools, battle equipment as well as household and ornamental objects if they are classed. Rectangular graves have been surveyed. were conducted in the areas in Herlen as well as Tuul Rivers' basins of Tov aymag, Orhon valley as well as Tevsh mountain Bogd sums of Ovorhangay aymag the southern portion of the Dundgovi aymag, Herlen, Onon and Hurh The basins of rivers include Hentiy aymag, Eg river of Bulgan aymag, Monhhaan and Erdenetsagaan sums Suhbaatar aymag that is a an open steppe that is located in the eastern part of Mongolia as well as discovered and studied hundreds of graves that are rectangular.

Bronze Helmet (Bronze Age, 110-700 BC, Bulgan, Hutag-Ondor); "Pottery shreds" as well as "Necklace" (Late Bronze/Early Iron Age, 1200-600 BC, Ovorhangay, Harhorin)

Tombs are also tributes to the first time that was The Bronze as well as Iron Ages. There are many tombs within Mongolia as well as tombs located on the on the right bank of Harbuh river Dashinchilen Sum, Bulgan Aymag are being meticulously explored by research. Deer statues are stunning historic and historical monuments to the culture of tribes, clans, and clans who were living in the territory of Mongolia as well as Central Asia during the beginning of the Bronze and Iron armaments. In the present, about 700 deer statues are discovered across the World and about 550 of them come from the region of Mongolia.

Steel armaments production differs in each nation in the world at different times. Clans and tribes lived in Mongolia prior to the advent of the iron armaments period in the period 700-300 BC. In the early days, Mongolians made tools for work as well as battle weapons out of steel by utilizing techniques for casting iron ore and producing steel axes, daggers, mattocks, knifes and nails. In the course of analyzing and defining multiple questions of life and culture of the people who lived in the early the iron armouring period in Mongolia tombs of certain types were excavated and studied on Chandmani mountain, which is located close to Ulaangom town. Uvs Aymag are important and significant.

Map of the Rock Drawings of Mongolia

ANCIENT STATES

In the 3000th year around BC even though the political system and writings had barely come into existence on the land in Central Asia, many nomads hunter provinces, herdsmen and hunters each with its own unique culture, were living on the territory of Mongolia. The societies of these provinces was growing through the final stage of its ancient structure and progressed to a period of history that established the civil and cultural society of the nomadic tribes. A large number of tribes and provinces came together from the Provinces.

Hunnu State at the time of 209 BC, Modun Shaniu (king) who was the ruler of the Hunnu Aymags, created the Hunnu State in 209 BC, and by combining and ruling 24 provinces belonging to the Hunnu state. They became prosperous and powerful in the 3rd century BC and founded their own state at first, in the ancient nomadic regions. Since they were the ancestors of the Mongols It is believed that the state they established was the first state of the Mongol nomadic people. The Palace of Modun Shaniu of the Hunnu State was located at the Valley of Orhon River, Hangay mountain ranges. Hunnu was surrounded by the Great Wall to the South, Baigal (Baikal) Lake in North, Il Tarvagatay Mountains to the west, and

Korea towards the east. In the wake of internal wars as well as the erratic practices implemented by the Han Dynasty, Hunnu State was divided into two sections in 53, and afterward, it was conquered and then sacked in 93 by Xianbi State in 93. The aristocratic inherited segment was used to rule the Hunnu state, but it influenced the the affinity structure as well as leaders of county and tribes had been retained. Hunnu State was divided into 3 sections. Hunnu State was divided into three sections, including western, central and eastern in addition to having the decimal system of organizational. The basis of Hunnu's farming and economics included hunter-gatherers, livestock management and farming of crops. They believed in shamanism, and they developed a script that was a significant contribution to the growth of nomadic culture as well as literary. Cultural and historical treasures are preserved throughout Mongolia to this day.

Xianbi State following the Hunnu's State, Xianbi people derived from the ancient Dunhu rule over Mongolia in the late the 1st century. They were comprised of Mongolian tribes and clans from central Asia and were integrated into Hunnu State. Hunnu State. Around 150, the Tanishihuai family of a former military officer from Xianbi joined the entire Xianbi provinces. The province was split into three components: West, East and Center and was governed by 12 different dominions. The middle in the 3rd century the Xianbi provincial federation fell and divided into a number of independent counties. In their place, Muyun as well as Toba provinces formed their own state on the territory of present-day Inner Mongolia and Northern China and remained in existence for quite a length of period of. While they still had the tribal system in the Xianbi society, differences in social status were quickly gaining momentum and developed in law of the state and the development of civilization. Following the Xianbi state's creation, writing scripts, education in economics and culture became more established. The script writing style was identical to ancient scripts that were written on wooden boards like the Hunnu people. They had a calendar that was named for 12 animals, and were a part of a shamanic religious system. They loved songs, poetry and music.

Jujan State The name has been mentioned in the past from the 4th century onwards. They created their own state within the borders of Mongolia and were derived of Hunnu, Dunhu and Xianbi Aymags. From the fourth to fifth Centuries A certain man named Shelun emerged of the Jujan

Aristocrats and conquered his neighbours and founded his own state, the Jujan State in the year 402. The palace of the Jujan King was located within the proximity of Hangay mountains. It was divided into three sections: western, central and eastern, and was governed by the decimal system of government or. In the aftermath of Shelun's death the state was functioning for about 140 years, and later was destroyed by the internal conflicts and revolts fought by the Tureg Aymags. The State was dispersed in the year 555. The state was much more advanced in terms of social structure than other state that was nomadic. The State had a shamanic faith similar to other states. In the end, Buddhism was spread out. The state and the other practices inherited from the Jujan people were passed down over generations.

Gold Vessels (Turkish period, Arhangay, Hashaat, Hoshoo Tsaydam, NMM)

Tureg State was established after Jujan, Tureg established the State in the country of Mongolia. Tureg aymags were as part of Hunnu Power. Hunnu Power. In the time of Jujan rule they made irons, and made tribute to Jujan rulers. The middle of the sixth century Buman an aymag ruler from Tureg aymag, was able to unite all of the subordinate counties and tribes that were subject to the rule of Jujan state. Buman was elevated to the rank of in the rank of "El" Khaan. He then established his own state, the Tureg State which was in existence for around 100 years, and was later under the control of Tan Dynasty for about 50 years. Then, at the close of the 6th century the country was hit by a massive revolt led by Tureg Aristocrats Kutulug and Tonyukuk, who reestablished Tureg State. Tureg State. From that point it has been the Tureg State was in constant conflict with the Chinese Tan Dynasty, defending its independence. But in 745 in 745, as the internal conflicts that befell the Tureg State got worse the state was beset by rebellions led by Uighur Aymags, and furthermore they seized power and it was the time that Tureg State was destroyed. The Tureg population developed the ancient nomadic culture from Central Asian nomads and left their cultural and economic heritages.

Koltegin statue head (Turkish period, Arhangay aymag, Hoshoo Tsaydam, NMM)

Uighur State they derived from Tureg nomadic tribes that were part of the ancient Altaic Language group. In the past, Chinese documents mentioned that the people who were ancestors to Uighur populace were referred to as Dinlin, Dili, Tele and finally Uighur (Huyhu) as of the 5th century. Since they were using the steel carts that had tall wheel, they would be referred to as "Gaogu" that was tall carters. The 8th century, during the time that Peilo Khaan took over, Uighur state defeated Tureg State and established Uighur State. Uighur State. The palace of Uighur Khaan was located at the Orhon River valley and called Black fortress. Following Peilo Khaan's reign, Moyunchur Khaan was the ruler of the Uighur state. He expanded his boundaries, which included Baigal Lake to the north and Great desert Govi to the south. In the end, the Uighur State was overrun by Kyrgyzs from Yenisei in 840. Some people settled in Turkistan. In addition to preserving nomadic customs they also cultivated their own culture. Uighur settled in settlements, and they were better developed than other nomads.

Remains from the Uighur the period between 8 and 9th century AD, Arhangay aymag, Hotont sum (NMM)

Khitan State they merged from an ancient Dunhu people who are similar to Mongols. The Khitan's name Khitan was first mentioned in the late history of the state at the close of the 4th century. Ambagyan the leader of Khitan altered a policy for presidium selection every 3 years. Additionally, he established an order of succession in the event that he was to take over the Khaan's position changed was passed down from generations. In addition, he founded Khitan state, which was created by the union of eight provinces that were once part of the old one. Ambagyan and his successors defeated the nomads of neighboring regions and sixteen counties from north of China. This is how Khitan turned into a major power, and it was dubbed the Great Liao State.

Ceramics and porcelain fragments man, 10-11th century (NMM)

The Khitan authority consists of around 50 provinces and nations and was split into north, south north, and foreign areas. Between 1118 and 1125, Zurchid people under Khitan's yoke, dissolved the Khitan state. They were in collaboration with the Sung Dynasty of China. The Khitan state was comprised of various populations in terms of both social and economic development. The educational and social development of Khitan inhabitants were better than those of the earlier nomadic tribes. They had a significant influence on the socio-cultural advancement of Mongol and Hamnigan inhabitants of the vast areas in Central as well as Eastern Asia.

Materials for construction, 10-11th century (NMM)

The Mongol AYMAGS and TRIBES during the period of 11-12th century. The 11-12th Centuries and the development of social relations of the Mongol tribal groups as well as aymags grew and also became more politically. Researchers have classified Mongols who lived at that time to be "Forest inhabitants" and "Steppe nomads". In the 12th century, there were large, independent counties and provinces of Mongolia such as Hamag Mongol, Jalayr, Taichuud, Merged and Naiman. Based on these, Hamag Mongol was becoming to be the leader of the other. Hamag Mongol used to comprise two major aymags, Nirun as well as Darligin. While Mongols were scattered, forming numerous aymags in the between the 12-13th century, they were being embraced by their lifestyle, styles, language, customs and cultural.

THE GREAT MONGOL STATE

In 1206, an important event within the historical background of Mongolia which led to the establishment of the Great Mongol State by Chinggis Khaan, who unified all the dispersed Mongol provinces to establish the state. Temuujin (Chinggis Khaan) was born in 1162 was the child of Esuhey Baatar, the leader of the Hamag Mongols. He became an orphan in the age of five his own hardships, but he was able to overcome them as well as the violence of enemies.

Chinggis Khaan (1162-1227)

In the beginning, he formed a relationship to Togoril the leader of the Hereid Aymag, which was a powerful force during the time so that he could strengthen his troops. It was his primary goal to restore an alliance with the Hamag Mongol headed by his father. Following the demise of his father Esuhey the clans split up Temuujin and his siblings.

In 1180, he joined Gurvan Merged people alongside Togoril and Jamuha. They they defeated them and released his queen Borte and others who had been detained by the. Then, he took over the Taichuud Aymag, and some of Jadran individuals were part of the Hamag Mongol. Therefore, Temuujin became by the Khaan Hamag Mongols in 1189 and during a ceremony which was held in Hoh Lake in Har Zurh Temuujin was elevated to the highest title, Chinggis Khaan.

Mongolian Black and White Standards

Through overcoming numerous difficulties such as wars and fighting and wars, he reunited all Mongols roots and was The Khaan (King) for all Mongols. The name was later given to the Great Mongol Empire. Chinggis Khaan paid a lot of attention to ensure the internal power of governing of the nation and created the decimal system, which was divided into ten thousand and thousands of organizational systems. The thousands military regime, also known as "Myangat", he aimed to increase the strength of Khaan's system of state control and utilize the capabilities of economics. The systems of the thousands were different from one another, for example the external and internal militants. The Myangat within the internal Myangat comprised respectable soldiers while the external Myangat comprised of regular herdersmen. The Hishigten (honorable soldiers) that were controlled or punished by Chinggis Khaan formed the mainstays of the army. The establishment of honorable soldiers was intended to make the Great Mongol State powerful and solid. Under the leadership of Chinggis Khaan organisations like "Setsediyn Huralday" (Palate of Wise) as well as "Ih Huralday" (Palate of Lords) were created and also. The Setsediyn Huralday was able to offer advice, while the Ih Huralday debated and resolved important issues on the organization of battles, and was elevated to Chinggis Khaan's singing. The primary legal system that governed the Great Mongol state was "Ih Zasag" which included the an explanation of the rights of the Great Mongol State, crowning the Khan title, calling the Ih Huralday in communication with other countries, the citizens obligation to serve and hunting finances, tax levies as well as succession to families. When the Great Mongol State was established that was bordered by Baikal Lake to the north, Great Hyangan Range to the east, the Great Hyangan Range to the Great wall to the south as well as the Altay Ranges to the west and covering vast areas that were previously scattered ended and the Mongolian nations became single state reign. The creation of the Great Mongol Power was an integration into the Mongolian society and was the catalyst to create The Great Mongol Empire. Chinggis's achievements and efforts Khaan been the catalyst for introducing the name Mongol into the world, and Mongols became part of our world's history.

Battle of Nahu Gun Mountain, 1204 (Fragment of painting NMM)

Battle on "Nahu-Gun" Mountain In 1204 The aristocracies from Jadran, Merged, Hereid, Dorvon Oirad, Tatar, Hatigan and Saljiud who were defeated by Mongolian tribes as well as Tayan Khan of the Naiman tribe joined forces in battle against Chinggis Khaan. Even though they were heavily outnumbered, Chinggis Khaan's forces won. The fight took place on Nahu-Gun Mountain, Bulgan aymag.

THE GREAT MONGOL EMPIRE

Following the establishment and maintenance of the Great Mongol state at the beginning of the 13th century Chinggis Khaan began large-scale combat operations across Asia as well as Europe. The main objective of the conflict was to guarantee protection for foreigners for the Great Mongol state, to extend its boundaries, increase its status as a formidable force and consolidate the its economic and political power. the Mongolian ruling class.

The Mongolian rulers first attached states that were in some way to their Great Mongol state, tried to establish alliances against it, but did not pay attention to the state, and organized conspiracies. Thus, they initially first, established the Xia State in Tangud in 1205 before they totally conquered the nation in 1207.

Mongolian armored soldier's coat made of mail from the 13th-14th centuries (NMM)

Mongolian armor for soldiers, iron. 13-14th century (NMM)

By using diplomatic means, Chinggis Khaan subjugated Uighurs from eastern Turkistan in the year 1209. In 1210, Chinggis Khaan was preparing to attack Jin State in Zurchid and departed for the Jin State of Zurchid with his massive army in the year 1211. A large army, led by Zev famous general, cut through the Chuulalt Haalga (present Zhangjiakou, close to Beijing) and captured Tsavchaal (Juyong Pass) which was a strong threat to Jin State. Jin State. Chinggis Khaan's army wiped out 30000 troops of Jin State during the time of Hebei province in China in the year 1211; and by the following year, several ports and fortresses were taken over. Elui-Luge, the chief of the previous Khitan State which was under the control of Jin State and was successful in his fight against Jin State and Chinggis Khaan. Even though the king of Jin State attempted to fight with Chinggis Khaan and cooperate with Tangud but it ended up being an unsuccessful effort because Tangud was subdued by Mongol forces. in 1213 Chinggis Khaan divided his vast army into 3 parts and then invaded Jin State and surrounded its capital city Chundu (present Beijing).

Mongolian soldier's armored shoes, and gear, 14th century (NMM)

The king in a panic of Jin State wished to give lots of presents and his daughter, along with 500 children and women to Chinggis Khaan for their friendship. Thus, the Chinggis Khaan were withdrawn and Jin State was repressed. Following the battle Chinggis Khaan dispatched messengers to Sung State of China and determined to form a relationship with the Sung State of China but the messengers had been held up by Jin and were in the process of in the process of preparing for war, and transferring its capital city, Kaifeng, to south Kaifeng.

Cauldron 13th century (NMM)

Being aware of this, Chinggis Khaan joined to the Jin State at the time of 1214. He the capital city was Chundu in addition to continuing the invading process. In the end, Chinggis was forced to return home and was given the responsibility of invasion to take over his former home, the Jin State, to his general Muhulay. One reason behind his return was to get ready for the conquest the region of Middle Asia, without delay. In the end, an essential tactic utilized by Mongolian conquerors under Chinggis Khaan wasn't to allow the adversaries to join forces in order to take on one at a time in order to make use of the both the military and financial resources of those countries that were occupied to fight in the future wars.

Arrowheads from Mongolian soldier (NMM)

Prior to launching an attack on Khwarizm Chinggis Khaan sent 20 thousand soldiers, with General Zev ZEV Har Khitan (western Liao) situated between the Great Mongol State and Khwarizm to attack in 1218. Zev general as well as his men declared to the people in Har Khitan that Mongolian troops did not have the right to sack normal people, anyone would enjoy the right to practice their preferred religion, but they would be able to punish rebels and thefts. In the time of Zev, the the natives of Har Khitan practiced the Muslim faith, while the Huchulug leaders were Buddhists. They didn't approve of the

Huchulug rule, so they accept the declaration of General Zev. Thus it was the Mongolian forces were no longer in their territory in the Har Khitan State.

In the following years, he was occupied the valley of Amu-Dariya River west of Afghanistan, Bukhara and Iran and finally reached Khwarizm State situated at a commercial route that connected China, Mediterranean sea, India and Southern Russia. In the end, the capture and execution of 450 traders, along with 500 camel caravans escorted to Utrar by Chinggis Khaan towards Utrar city, was the main reason for the invasion of Khwarizm from the Mongols.

Mongolian massive army, under Chinggis Khaan attacked Khwarizm between 1219 and 1224. It took over cities such like Utrar, Benakent, Hagent, Buhara, Zarik, Nur, Zareshan, Urgench, Samarkand, Balkh, Mery and Nishapur after which in

1224, the Khwarizm State was conquered. The brave warrior against the Mongolian forces was Jelal-Ad-Din who was a child of Mohammed. He was able to defeat 30000 troops under the command of Shihihutug Chinggis Khaan's soldiers swept the battlefield clean of their troops. He fled into India after which he reached Peres by crossing the Indus the river on horseback and fighting up to 1231.

There was a report Chingges Khaan greatly appreciated Jelal-Ad-Din for his bravery and encouraged his soldiers to follow his example.

The troops, led by Zev Subeedey and Zev Subeedey arrived in Azerbaijan before they entered Georgia to defeat Georgian 60000 troops led by Lasha the king. They also overcame Caucasian mountains and beat troops of Russian Kingships along the Kalka River. In addition they defeated the

Mongols took over Bulgaria before returning home to their home country.

The main forces of Mongolian forces invaded Middle Asia and Eastern Europe but were returned to their home country in 1225. Xi Xia State of Tangud, which was located under the rule of Mongolia was not able to assist Mongolian soldiers in Chinggis Khaan's Western War Campaign and, more notably, the rulers made insulting remarks and used as a time frame that Mongolian soldiers went in the west for battles and battles, they arranged to join Mongolia and attempted to disintegrate the Mongolian state by colluding in secret with Jin State. When the truth was exposed Chinggis Khaan gathered 100,000 troops and began to invade the Tangud in the Ezenee River's direction and defeated the current Gurvan Sayhan Mountains, at the start of 1226.

The two sides fought fiercely between the two sides. Even though Chinggis Khaan was killed on the 25th August 1227, his generals fought the battle and eventually dissolved the Tangud state eventually.

Ogoodey Khaan (1186-1241)

Following Chinggis Khaan's departure and his sons, Chinggis Khaan's succeeding heirs Ogoodey (third child of Chinggis Khaan), Guyug, Monh and Hubilay (grandson of Chinggis Khaan) carried on the war which was waged in Asia as well as Europe and founded the Great Mongol Empire, occupying all of China, Central, Eastern and Middle Asia, and Eastern Europe.

Hubilay Khaan (1215-1294)

The Mongolian victory destroyed several cities in Asia as well as Europe as well as killed thousands of people as well as depressed populations of conquered nations.

A painting that depicts a war between the Hubilay Khaan's army against Japanese (NMM). Japanese (NMM)

Scientists have proved there had been a new developments in economics, politics and cultural aspects within the boundaries that were part of the Great Mongol Empire situated throughout Asia as well as Europe and was founded with Chinggis Khan. Horseback rides across areas belonging to the Great Mongol Empire was the most efficient communication device. Westerners and easterners utilized horses to complete their errands, ensuring that the relations between Great Mongolian Empire, Asia as well as Europe was increasing beyond the recognition. Mongols introduced coins and banknotes in circulation and made it possible for handcrafts, commercial manufactures and astronomy centres to flourish. The beautiful and elegant buildings constructed in the time of Il-Khaan Oziyt (1304-1311) as well as Abu (1316-1325) today becoming stunning architecture-related monuments to Persia. Along with the law and regulations enacted by Mongolia have had a positive impact on educational and legal practices of countries that were occupied.

Pottery vessels discovered in the water (Battle between the Hubilay Khaan's troops against Japanese) Japanese) (NMM)

In the past, a rigid military structure, strategies, battle tactics, and strategies employed by Mongol troops, guided to the development of innovative ideas within the field of military in a variety of countries. Visitors were surprised that there were temples as well as churches that represented different types of faiths like Buddhism, Christianity, Muslim and Daoism all in one city that could be understood and the freedom to choose a religion was wide-ranging.

Thus it is clear that the Great Mongol Empire founded by Chinggis Khaan as well as his successors had a major impact on the development of history, and left indelible marks on historical record of the world. Chinggis Khaan was an incredibly brilliant general and politician who was admired not just in Mongolia but also throughout the world's the history of. Chinggis Khaan also brought the nomadic Mongols famous throughout the global the world's history. In the end Chinggis Khaan has been immortalized as a symbol for the respectability of the entire group of Mongols.